For sharing with Yale
(Board of Directors

B.W. Pursecki

PRAISE FOR *WEALTH AND CLIMATE COMPETITIVENESS*

The importance of narrative and storytelling comes through loud and clear in Piasecki's new book. His sourcing is rich and wonderful on competition and social needs. Like in his prior books, we can hear the nascent tales of today becoming the truisms of tomorrow.

—Dominic Emery, former chief of staff of bp
and distinguished engineer, Board Member

Piasecki is a master storyteller of both history and personal insight. Informative, persuasive, delightful—this is a great tale rendered in personal narrative like a Henry David Thoreau and Piasecki's heroes Churchill and Orwell. This book is full of insights in each passage, and the complete short manifesto reads with persuasive rage.

—Ken Strassner, former senior executive
of Kimberly Clark, Board Member

What I love most about this book is Piasecki's passionate appeal to shared feelings about our near future. As in his prior books, Piasecki challenges you to grasp a broad array of history and literature in compelling prose designed for global translation. He will challenge you to change in ways you had not considered yet. Suddenly these better selves seem both logical and justified in his life summary book.

—Ira Feldman, Attorney/Founder of Adaptation Leader.

"From Knoke's *Bold New World* in 1996 to Bogle on the *Soul of Capitalism* in 2005 and then to Piasecki's own *World Inc.* in 2007, great books have been released on mixing the needs of the new world with capitalism. In this new book, Bruce Piasecki offers a dramatically engaging manual and a new generation manifesto for the ages. In this regard, Bruce is the current successor to Peter Drucker.

—Darryl Vernon Poole, accountant,
CEO newsletter founder, and cultural historian

WEALTH AND CLIMATE COMPETITIVENESS

The New Narrative on Business and Society

BRUCE PIASECKI

RODIN
BOOKS™

Hardcover ISBN: 978-1-957588-16-2
eBook ISBN: 978-1-957588-17-9

PUBLISHED BY RODIN BOOKS INC
666 Old Country Road
Suite 510
Garden City, New York 11530

www.rodinbooks.com

Book and cover design by Alexia Garaventa

Manufactured in the United States of America

RODIN
BOOKS™

OTHER TITLES BY BRUCE PIASECKI

CONTENTS

ACKNOWLEDGMENTS

Without the steady routines of working with my editor of six books, Peter Lynch, this book on wealth would have remained much longer. Without the brilliant improvements suggested by my agent and owner of www.scottmeredith.com, Arthur Klebanoff, this book on climate and social movements would not have had the impact we anticipated. Arthur helped this writer see many uses in the realm of corporates, individuals, and governments.

And again, without the love of my daughter and wife, I would not have had the routines that allow such books at all.

WHAT IS CLIMATE COMPETITIVENESS?

Over the last century and more, there has been a tense relationship between business and society, and how they interact with each other. A set of prejudices on both sides lead to a general understanding that business and society were at odds, especially when it came to our planet and the effects of climate change.

However, by the end of the twentieth century, a new social contract began to emerge. Business and society, wealth and the commonwealth, began to be perceived as intimately related. With this change, I believe that we have reached a turning point toward a better future, which is rooted in a new concept: climate competitiveness.

What is climate competitiveness? At its core, climate competitiveness is about using your business, with all the tools of capitalism, to address and respond to large social demands.

Climate competitiveness is a comprehensive corporate response to a range of issues surrounding business and society. It is larger than the kinds of corporate strategy seminars you hear at the best business schools. Climate competitiveness involves the blending of private scientific and market knowledge, along with corporate culture and ambitions, to create solutions years ahead of when governments might try to solve them with taxes or regulatory demands. And by creating such solutions, you can put your company or firm years ahead of its competition.

Climate competitiveness engages the more positive forces in social change. This happens without revolution or social chaos. In fact, the opposite happens. Societies across the nations re-achieve the lost balance between business and society, between wealth and the commonwealth, in ways that redistribute wealth to those that are climate competitive (while those who aren't lose).

But this is not simply an altruistic mission. (Although those who approach it with a sincere goal of benefitting society will succeed best.) The relationship between the financial success of a business and its efforts to create social good are intertwined. Creating innovative solutions requires capital in order to research and fund the efforts. And the solutions developed must bring in further capital in order to fund the next innovations.

Climate competitiveness is about balancing the cash flow needs of innovation with the arts of competitive frugality. People need enough excess in their lives to be creative and to know their roles in the expanding, globalized world. In the same way, the great value-based corporates need enough excess in their firms to afford the major innovations. You can see how this approach re-engineers the pursuit of profit to a way that benefits business and society alike.

That is what has been missed too often since the last financial meltdown: The people who are profiting also believe in investing along the lines of environmental, social and governance metrics (ESG). This ESG movement is now dominating oil valuations. While it is still a method of some controversy, ESG has demonstrative social value in the way major firms position themselves for change. I find this hard to write about because every day the issues are hotly debated in the press and in the boardrooms on which I serve; yet what is clear is that winners are on the path of climate competitiveness, and losers are those refusing the new ESG investment monies now available.

Now, climate competitiveness may mean different things for different companies. For bp, it means a fundamental shift in energy sales and selection. At Trane, it means bringing the outside megatrends inside, through human resources retraining.

Regardless of how you define it in your field, the lesson is that the future worth of your firm lies in finding your role on this path of climate competitiveness.

Climate competitiveness involves a responsible, steady, resolve-based focus on lessons derived from human behavior and social movements. This book is designed to give you a deep understanding of the changed landscape we now face, and how you can resolve to embrace climate competitiveness to drive your success, and the success of our world.

ON MONEY, PEOPLE, AND RULES

When you get down to essences, most business success depends on the smart alignment of money, people, and rules.

How you define your staff, its functions, and its accountability, is the first high-octane fuel in the engine of business success. In short, how you manage your people, find brilliant deputies, and structure your differentiated organization remains key. In my firm, the people element was critical.

I started my journey aligning money, people, and rules with few funds. I succeeded because of the talent of individual teams, not big loans. Money is not just the world of finance, as the best firms are not debt bound but frugal in a competitive sense. "Wealth" we find in people, social networks, and professional communities and organizations. Wealth is human worth made operational. In this book, we examine the arts of competitive frugality both in principle and in case examples.

The "rules part" is where the social movements and governments come in. Issues such as toxic waste contamination, or the vaccine crisis of the last pandemic, or climate change require the heavy feet of government to set the rules by which competition for innovation begins and ends.

Yet you cannot solve the climate crisis only with government mandates. That is sharpening only half of a pair of scissors. To cut through these issues of the many greenhouse gas emitters in transportation, big pharma, buildings, and hospitals, we need to be more clever than simply be pro-regulation. We cannot strangle the neck of innovation, or the inherent powers in private and corporate wealth.

This book offers eighteen related passages that offer the new narrative on business and society, which will allow us to compete in a carbon- and capital-constrained world. We have centered each of the passages on two historic insights, one on the past mistakes and the other pointing to future solutions on wealth, its prejudices, and the climate crisis.

THE FIVE PREJUDICES

Many of the central concerns of the twenty-first century —racial inequity, white supremacy movements, greater inclusiveness of diverse peoples—are rooted in facing and overcoming prejudices. Another of our great challenges— the role of wealth and its relationship to the needs of the commonwealth—is also driven by a set of prejudices that have grown and evolved over the last two centuries. That is the puzzling domain of this text.

This set of prejudices—five that I've discerned as recurrent and damaging—has led us to believe impossible things, such as the only way to address the climate crisis is through draconian global mandates, a set of mandates not likely in our world of war, limited upward mobility, and serious public health problems. Look at how this is summed up in the new report on the climate crisis:

> On March 20, 2023, the Intergovernmental Panel on Climate Change (IPCC) re-

leased its Sixth Assessment Report. IPCC's research clearly shows that human activity has unequivocally driven climate change. As a result, the world is currently on track to fall short of achieving the 1.5°C (2.7°F) limit from the 2015 Paris Agreement, and unless significant actions are taken immediately, we will exceed 2°C (3.6°F). Countries and companies must make drastic changes in energy consumption, land use, and infrastructure now in order to limit the most severe impacts of climate change.

(Source: IPCC Report, United Nations webpages, *New York Times* summaries)

While this quote sums up the position of the most prestigious group of scientists on the issue of climate in the world, it only states the problems, with no doable solutions in hand. These reports do not delve into how wealth, innovation, and corporate innovators generate the solutions and their paths in society. That immense absence is what this book offers to fill and to explore with a range of readers.

You can find a thousand policy and legal citations about the urgency of the climate crisis, yet only a few of them provide the path of how these solutions will be achieved. From the early works of Bill McKibben and the scientists at NOAA, most of the works have been apocalyptic in describing the harm, with little attention to the path to climate competitiveness. With only warnings, you just cut the problems in half. While many rely on regulatory reform to advance the case on climate solutions, that is only half the pair of scissors. You also need the back legs of investments and corporate strategy to get where we all need to be by 2035 and 2040.

Each of us will now confront the consequences of climate change in our lives, the lives of our family, our health, and in our firms. In that confrontation, we argue for a new, more hopeful, narrative on how business and society interact.

Picture this new narrative as a stern elephant moving forward. This metaphor of social history involves the four legs of **technology** (often autonomously issued onto the world), **capital markets** (a fierce set of individual or corporate self-interests measured in the short term), **government mandates** and the laws and policies, and the world of innovative **corporate strategy.**

Technology

Capital Markets

Government Mandates

Corporate strategy and innovation

I am a social historian, and corporate change agent. In my firm, **www.ahcgroup.com**, I've worked in teams, across the last forty years, marching, in a series of unrelated projects, alongside these four legs in different consulting and government advisory roles. This book sums up the findings in one place for a new generation of business and social leaders.

We define climate competitiveness as the path forward that benefits the world as it strengthens each leg of the elephant of our shared history.

THE DISTORTIONS PREJUDICES CREATE

Yet our grounds for hope are not based on blind hope. We are aware of the retarding forces—the prejudices—that have tripped up proper responses to wealth creation and the climate crisis.

Instead, we start by explaining, using some exceptional corporate cases, why a set of five domineering popular prejudices, from 1900 to 2020, have held up any real progress on climate action.

In the second half of this book, we explain why these historically resisting forces are about to be changed for the better through investment trends, changes in climate policy and taxation.

If you get too entrenched in the debates generated by these prejudices, you sometimes miss the forest for the trees. That is why we think it wise and effective to note the distortions that these prejudices create. In addition, we find we can provide some early compelling examples. The sequence of passages enables this dual observation: both the history of the past mistakes made by the prejudices on how companies work, and the view forward, i.e., how the elephant proceeds through decades.

At times, we will descend more deeply into a thicket, what I like to call a "dense opportunity." Do not think of this as a descent into a meaningless rabbit hole. Instead, like a swift eagle diving, we will fly over the contours of popular assumptions, focusing on five recurring prejudices that have driven the increasingly troubled relationship between the wealth in our nation and the commonwealth of our people.

In the end, we show a path forward to balance that relationship, and restore our basic civics, which unfortunately have been broken.

This book sums up the principles and the findings in one place for current business and policy leaders, as it addresses the narrative that might stimulate the everyday citizen and reader.

PRIVATE WEALTH AND CORPORATE SPRAWL

Much of social history focuses on the private wealth of individuals, their dynastic families, and the corporations made by such titans of industry. Yet beneath this corporate sprawl, you can find examples of more frugal leadership, and answers to our climate crisis. I say this based on having served in my firm's team nearly one fifth of Fortune 500 companies in my forty-two years of earnings. See more on the firm at www.ahcgroup.com.

My entire career as business owner and business and society writer have centered on this concept of changing firms—mastering their technical market and personnel needs—with the idea of social response capitalism. "Social response capitalism," as defined at length in my book, *World Inc* (2007, Sourcebooks), is about the better alignment of money, people, and rules to address social

needs, such as the needs for more efficient and afford-
able transportation, and for addressing climate storms
and the emissions leading to climate change as best as
humanly possible.

Here, in brief, are the five prejudices you will find
dissected in this book:

1. **THE RICH AS "ROBBER BARON":** Since the discovery of oil, and its boom economics, an image of
   wealth has emerged as a set of overweight robber barons with big insulting cigars. This image dominated
   the debates on regulation, control, and purpose. In
   this visual, these "men" work behind closed doors,
   in rooms filled with cigar smoke, with other capitalists, no press present, no government oversight, and
   achieve abundant results.

2. **CIVIL DISOBEDIENCE AND PROTEST AS "SO-
   CIALISM":** Articulate social critics like Henry
   David Thoreau suggested the voice of the commonwealth is best felt when workers shove their
   wooden shoes into the machinery of exploitations.
   His work on civil disobedience influenced Gandhi
   in India and Europe, and Martin Luther King Jr.
   As these protest efforts evolved, they began to be associated with shrill, insistent, sometimes violent acts
   of "socialism." Often lost was the understanding that
   a Thoreau-like examination of capitalism and wealth
   are the birth of social movements that matter more
   and more, as governments are unable to control the
   rampant globalization of capitalism.

3. **CAPITALISTS AS THE "FITTEST" BIRDS OF PREY:**
As the American model became more universally fa-
vored following the World Wars, there grew a parallel and somewhat hidden prejudice that the wealthy
are like birds of prey, roaming thousands of miles
for their kill. By the end of the twentieth century,
these capitalists will have built elaborate lobbying,
government affairs, and public affairs departments
to make their flight more like that of stealth bomb-
ers. Along the way, the great works of Darwin,
Freud, and Marx became cooked into justifications
that one is wealthy because they are the "fittest"
both in the market, in their minds (Freud), and in
their control of the means of production (Marx).
For decades, this prejudice produced a profoundly
disruptive myth regarding the interplay of wealth
and the commonwealth. These fine-feathered nineteenth-century writers prepared us to stay fixed in
this age of climate change and industrialism.

4. **WEALTH DESERVES LUXURY:** One lasting prejudice
from the Roaring Twenties is the notion that wealth
deserves excessive luxury—a kind of conspicuous
life of idle and wasteful consumption. While the
wealthy glide by in beautiful silks and yachts, the
poor can barely account for their birth papers and
are without watches. By the late twentieth-century,
there is a sense of "the bonfire of the vanities" as
captured by Tom Wolfe in his dramatically incisive
and sportive novel. The classic Greek and Scottish

Enlightenment understanding—that wealth brings social benefits and vice versa in an elaborate osmotic balance—becomes a set of extremes: the rich and the poor. Although the facts show that creative people coming from poverty can move into education and social wealth, many in this country believe that the average American lives a lesser life, more a cog in the machine of progress.

5. **WEALTH VERSUS THE COMMONWEALTH AS STATUS QUO:** As a result of the previous prejudices, by the late twentieth and early twenty-first centuries, the separation between the wealthy and the commonwealth is seen as natural and self-justified. Since wealth is considered a self-justifying force, its displays lead to the fabulous birth of the "leisure class."

Soon Elon Musk will be running three or four ventures at once, as if he is the sole operator of those complex technical ventures; and Jeff Bezos will be calling his hundreds of thousands of workers "Amazonians" in his letters to the stockholders. This last prejudice makes the end of the twentieth century especially turbulent, enabling the rise of anti-commonwealth leaders like Boris Johnson in England and Donald Trump in the United States.

Positively, there is a subtle recognition in dozens of nations that there is a new kind of social-response capitalism, where firms use their pricing, talents, technologies, and management savvy to compete on social needs for the elderly, for social mobility, and for a cleaner energy system. Yet there remains a strong anti-commonwealth theme in popular politics.

This approach provides the explanation as to why we now have a historic opportunity before us to step "beyond" the petrochemical treadmill into a cleaner and more vivid future for many.

RICH AS ROBBER BARONS —A LASTING NINETEENTH- CENTURY PREJUDICE

Edwin Drake discovered oil for profit in 1859. But it was the discovery of the Spindletop oilfield in Texas that launched the modern oil boom. Through the nineteenth century this caused the biggest extended boom of economic superabundance in human history. But it also led to a set of prejudices that caused a great divide between the wealthy and the commonwealth of the people, one we're still struggling to overcome today.

In stark contrast to this dominating prejudice of the corporate robber baron, let's look at a company (Trane Technologies) who has managed to overcome the disabling prejudices in our modern day. Trane secures its advantages over others in building and transportation and food delivery by competing for the path of climate competitiveness.

WHY TRANE TECHNOLOGIES IS AN EXCEPTION

Trane Technologies, a global firm of now over 50,000 technically gifted engineers and executives, is today's poster child for a rich stock that operates as a socially responsive capitalist organization. While the S&P Industrial Index rose in stock value nearly 250 percent during the days of the COVID pandemic, Trane's stock increased in value 408 percent. We have designed our case to focus on these five magnificent years of transformation and stock result.

As a social response firm, they did not fall prey to vague notions of corporate responsibility. Instead, they set their social aims, profitability, and talent pools around social trends that are more lasting than any given regional market trend. This allowed them to globalize their strategy in the States, in Asia, Africa, and elsewhere. Trane informed us of these developments firsthand, being an ongoing member of our firm's Corporate Affiliates program for nine years. They presented to our forty-two global firms claims in a confidential atmosphere.

Trane operates by making refrigerants with fewer climate emitting magnifiers, substantially less per unit of electricity consumed for air conditioning, refrigeration, or building temperature control. This proved critical in the years 2018 to 2023, the zone of change studied in this chapter. Trane sustained the nutritional value of large food trucks with their hyper-efficient truck "brains" (the refrigeration units above the truck itself); the brains, in fact, of most Wal-Marts and food trucks. They helped malls and supermarkets get smarter than ever on energy efficiency, for example, by using advanced computers to heat or cool a movie theater relative to the number of people who just purchased tickets. Why do they do that, and why do they operate in a transparent fashion, far distant from the robber barons of oil and gas?

The case of Trane proves that "sustainability" is not the only social value at hand. Rather, their story is about aligning finance, procurement, innovation, social responsibility, and human talent for sustained competitive advocacy. Without a doubt, such big moves in corporate strategy take resolve. Trane started by exploring the intersection of global megatrends with their old firm's innovation and talent capabilities. They did this through a complex set of outside experts, managed for years by Scott Tew, one of the executives in our Corporate Affiliates workshops.

- NYSE: TT
  - Began trading as an independent company in March 2020 following spin-off from Ingersoll Rand
  - 2019 Revenues: $13.0B (Est.)
  - Current Market Cap: $22.8B
  - 2019 Net Income: $1.4B

- 50,000 employees

- Headquartered in Ireland and Davidson, North Carolina

"As a world leader in creating comfortable, sustainable, and efficient environments, it's our responsibility to put the planet first."

—TRANE TECHNOLOGIES

Here is what this global corporation now looks like. We start with their miracle year of fiscal 2020, when they far excelled in value past the others in the S&P Industrials 500 index. We reveal both the two year foreground to this successful transition, and the few years after leading to today. But the emphasis is on how they did it.

What matters for climate and wealth is how the miracle began and matured, for it records the ways in which Trane took the outside world of megatrends inside, how they altered their firm to be a business in society, and began to profit in a world of climate impacts and needs. Here is a snapshot of Trane at the beginning of the transformation in 2019 and 2020 financials.

You can look up how much growth has occurred on the web in investment news from this starting point. The questions that remain center on what kind of thinking, or framing of world developments, did Trane undergo in order to break past the prejudices that had surrounded so many companies still addicted to the old petrochemical ways.

To answer this, we need to "contextualize" Trane in history and culture—so you can see how its size matters, and how astonishing its scale of transformation has become. Page 27 compares a relatively unknown Trane to the universal holder of popular brands Unilever, the long-standing equipment and earth moving giant CAT, and a growing fertilizer and food supply chain giant Nutrien. Here is the information we used in presenting the Trane case to bp over the last few years, developing a taste for

CONTEXTUALIZING TRANE

Company	Market Cap (as of 6/2020)	2019 Revenues	2019 Net Income	Employees
7RANE TECHNOLOGIES	$22.8B	$13.0B (Est.)	$1.4B	50K
Unilever	$143.43B	$51.98B	$5.625B	155K
CAT	$72.3B	$53.8B	$6.1B	102,300
Nutrien	$21.5B	$20.0B	$1.0B	22,300

the miracle of value and growth found in Trane on getting on the path of a smart and compounding climate response.

These are the accepted benchmarks that Trane uses, comparing itself to well-respected giants like Unilever and long held industrial giants like CAT. We (my six-person internal company research team and I) were surprised that they benchmarked another former client of ours, Agrium, which merged with another fertilizer giant around this time to become Nutrien. Trane looks at this range of achievers to make sure their governance systems are mature. Trane wanted to make sure they measured up to the leadership trends to the right world trends in their strategies. This is a form of advanced competition.

We are presenting here the 2019 and 2020 numbers, rather than current 2023 numbers, for many reasons. The change began then, and its value was manifest in the 2022 and 2023 stock values of Trane. Again, the purpose is to find the root cause of the miracle of transformation in the Trane case. How did this occur?

These are the years when Trane "took off" according to some of the wealth advisors such as Bank of America, Merrill Lynch, and even the conservative universal stockholders like TIAA CREF, and other named retirement annuities. While a great firm like Unilever leveled off some in stock value during the pandemic, Trane grew in all measures. Note how their CEO at the time, Michael W. Lamach, described these key pivotal sixty months:

A WORD FROM TRANE'S CHAIRMAN AND CEO

"Fundamentally, we excel **where global megatrends and sustainability intersect** with our innovation and capabilities. Today, 15% of the world's carbon emissions (CO_2e) come from heating and cooling buildings, and another 8% comes from global food loss. And these numbers are growing.

We are continually innovating to bend the curve on global warming. By 2030, we will reduce our customer's carbon emissions (CO_2e) by 1 gigaton by changing the way the world heats and cools buildings and moves refrigerated food, medicines and other perishables."

—**MICHAEL W. LAMACH,**
chairman and chief executive officer

The idea of "bending the curve on global warming" is what climate competitiveness requires. In sum, Trane institutionalized a "sustainable innovation" process (that is what they call their path to climate competitiveness, "sustainable innovation") that enables climate competitiveness—the union of technology, market forces, human talent, and timely embrace of new policy goals of governments. This pathway in Trane's case involved not only the CEO, Paul Caputo, their SVP of Strategy, Scott Tew and his executive external council, but also a strong new human resources executive and her team.

The Gigaton Challenge

We're reducing one gigaton of carbon emissions (CO_2e) from our customers' footprint by 2030. Join us.

HOW WE'LL DO IT

We're scaling technology, innovation and sustainability strategies and rethinking our supply chain to achieve carbon neutral operations.

OUR PROGRESS

21M

metric tons of CO_2e avoided over the past six years through the use of energy efficient and low emitting technologies

30+

countries where we are selling next generation solutions

ONE BILLION METRIC TONS

One Gigaton of CO_2e

We are committed to reduce our customer carbon footprint by one gigaton of CO_2e by 2030.

This is the largest customer climate commitment made by any B2B company, and our math shows that the reduction could equate to 25% of the world's annual emissions—or, the annual emissions of Italy, France and the UK combined.

ONE GIGATON OF $CO_2e=$

As a pure play climate innovator, we are uniquely positioned to lead a movement to reduce greenhouse gas (GHG) emissions.

And we're taking advantage of the opportunity in a big way. How big?

WHY WE NEED TO ADDRESS DECARBONIZATION

Aging Buildings
Large buildings are used longer than other buildings, and older buildings use more energy. The key to energy efficiency and greenhouse gas reduction is ensuring that these buildings can be maintained, retrofitted, and energy managed successfully.

Energy Intensity
Buildings consume about 40% of the energy produced in the United States. Additionally, a third of the building's energy use is from HVAC, and energy demand for cooling will more than triple by 2050

Carbon Emissions (CO_2e)
Approximately 15% of the world's carbon emissions (CO_2e) come from the heating and cooling of buildings. As urbanization accelerates and the world gets warmer, that figure could approach 25% by 2030.

Food Waste
If food loss and waste were its own country, it would be the third-largest greenhouse-gas emitter.

SPECULATIVE CAPITALISTS AS BIRDS OF PREY—A LASTING TWENTIETH-CENTURY PREJUDICE ON CLIMATE AND WEALTH

But in contrast to Trane, why do so many firms remain blinded by prejudices that do not allow such coordinated transformation? Why do so many mighty talented firms still fail, and why do many drive themselves into bankruptcy. In this book we are painfully aware that most firms do not change as Trane did. Instead, they flounder, and often fail. Their addictions are to the disabling prejudices framing this book. Unlike an alcoholic who cannot biologically break from their vices, these firms are locked in a nineteenth-century way of thinking about capital, capitalists, and society, a form of thinking developed during the boom decades of oil, which were not reshaped until now.

To see as a vivid exception to the corporate norms that ignore these climate issues, please recall the popular prejudices that Trane broke from. They always spoke about getting "off" the petrochemical treadmill whenever sensible.

I find it useful to use history and quotable writers to help regain perspective. It is important, for example, to explore two relatively unknown book writers, one of old and one of the legendary contemporary name, Gates. In doing this bird's eye view of oil history, and its distortion of civics, we will be able to help the new narrative get beyond the simple buzz words of "corporate purpose" or "corporate social responsibility." Trane operationalizes into business value and social result something more measurable than buzz words; hence, the financial stock results.

Yet how Trane generates this compounding mix of corporate and social wealth deserves further inspection from the backwards glance of history. Edwin E. Hale, referring to Henry Demarest Lloyd's *Wealth Against Commonwealth*, called it "as much an epoch-making book as *Uncle Tom's Cabin*." An epoch is a long time. Lloyd's book helps us see the need for a new narrative on business and society, since although his insights are accurate, his muckraking style does not jive well with our modern sense of wealth and society.

Published in 1894, Lloyd's book has a high style to it, where insights are granted more weight than empiricism.

It reads like a sermon combined with a literary lecture, with excited pauses and passages of profound implication. And, to my amazement, a few strong points remain significant to the pressures of a world like ours, which is seeking net-zero programs on global-warming emissions.

Lloyd was confronting a world that was starting to face great change from the boom in oil.

As you think back to Lloyd's day and his set of insights, imagine the remoteness of Texas when the gushing of oil began. If you remember when Texan cows roamed near the primitive rigs below, you will get a sense of how Trane is a twenty-first-century firm.

You can picture the rural scene in a Texas farmland where the early oil pumps were set next to the cattle and the homes. Yet the financial and political results were set far from Washington, DC, and the bankers of Manhattan. It first started as local booms, in many separate places. However, as Lloyd and I argue, it would come to harm civic stability in every neighborhood and state capitol in the United States.

Lloyd opens his muck-racking book with this striking passage:

> Nature is rich; but everywhere man, the heir of nature, is poor. Never in this happy country or elsewhere . . . has there been enough of anything for the people. Never since time began have all the sons and daughters of men been all warm, and all filled, and all shod and roofed.

In chapter 5, he writes:

> It was an American idea to "strike oil." Those
> who knew it as the slime of Genesis, or used
> it to stick together the bricks of the Tower of
> Babel, or knelt to it in the fire temples, were
> content to take it as it rose, the easy gift of
> nature, oozing forth, on brook or spring. But
> in America we struck it.

You can tell by the references to Genesis and the
Tower of Babel that Lloyd recognizes civic health is based
on a balancing of wealth and the commonwealth through
a set of facts "higher" than sheer booming in oil.

Lloyd's book was not the only one describing what
was to be true about oil economies. But it was one of the
first. He clearly notes that the discovery of petroleum had
the potential to distract many in society—in their pursuit
of quick wealth—from basic civic responsibilities.

"The higher facts" of the social contract—such as cultural restraint, rule of law in contracts, steady returns—
became secondary to the dictates of speculative boom
capitalism. The functional business dictates of restraint
began to fade in the age of oil.

What I find brilliant about Lloyd's early insights—
despite his heavy-handed design and style—can be found
in his chapter 14, "I want to make oil" and his chapter
23, "Freedom and the City." In these chapters you can
see how capitalism is based on a declaration of a business plan predicated on wicked and wild returns, without

specifics on how to achieve those returns. Lloyd also helps us see how the modern city is a byproduct of abundant oil. Lloyd demonstrates how many falsely concluded you cannot have great concentrated wealth in the cities without the black gold, forgetting the history of many past great cities that were not based on oil.

Lloyd's book forms the cornerstone of my main argument in the first ten passages of this book: As a result of this oil boom and the civic erosion it caused, the petrochemical treadmill now has all medicine, all science, all economies on its back—like a flipped beetle in your spring. The boom was so sustained, and it proved such a lasting gusher, that the force of the collective and dispersed wealth creations changed the basics of civic life.

We will see that the leaders and engineers making Trane into a 50,000 person, rapidly valued giant did not keep this popular presumption that oil would be endless, nor did they assume like Lloyd that change was unlikely. In stepping off the petrochemical treadmill, they stepped onto an early path to climate competitiveness.

Of course, this drawdown on our natural ecosystems is, in essence, larger than oil. It is too simple to say climate change is only the result of the Texas oil boom. The complete story includes coal, natural gas, and other extracted fossil fuels with high BTU value. What we say here in the "simplification of blame on oil" is true to all carbon emissions, nitrogen, ozone atmospheric problems, and to the earlier traditions of the impacts of acid rain.

In short, it is a simplification to cluster all the hundreds of greenhouse gas emissions magnifiers under the rubric of oil; yet it is also true that it was oil that allowed the development and use of all these industrial elements in our petrochemical treadmill.

The boom of oil led to a significant misalignment in our sense of risk and reward, where we discounted the future in a grand slam of the present. And this significant misalignment changed the American sense of the roles of government, which then rattled through the world from the United Kingdom to Saudi Arabia and throughout the globe. Oil became the nexus of our economy, and Texas was at the nexus of this first and ramifying set of changes. Even today, my visits to the Houston Oil Club reveal remnants of this Earth-changing attitude in the club members.

What is astonishing about Lloyd's book is that the great vast majority of executives running today's oil-based and petroleum chemicals firms still believe everything is fine, nothing is really broken in our views of nature, and that Lloyd is a kind of early idiot.

Massive corporate change, like that seen at Trane, only occurs when it reaches thousands of people in the firm.

Watch how alert to social and energy change Trane became. Trane's External Advisory Council on Sustainability is where this all started around 2013. During my interviews with some of the folks noted in the following list on page 41, they said things about civics and the dangers of a lazy view of energy in tone and fashion of Lloyd's muckracking diatribe, even though they were distinguished experts and capitalists.

TRANE TECHNOLOGIES

EXTERNAL ADVISORY COUNCIL ON SUSTAINABILITY

Roberta Bowman
SVP and Chief Sustainability Officer (retired), Duke Energy

Marian Chertow
Professor and Director, Industrial Environment Management Program, Yale University

Stuart Hart
Chair in Sustainable Business, University of Vermont, Author and Founder of Enterprise for Sustainable World

Peter Madden
CEO, Catapult Future Cities (Retired)

Bindu Lohani
EVP & Sustainable Finance Leader (retired), Asian Development Bank

George Bandy
CSO, Shaw (former); USGBC Chairman

Clause Stig Pederson
Head of Corporate Sustainability, Novozymes

Katherine Sierra
Senior Fellow, Brookings Institute

Daniel Vermeer
Professor & Exec Director, EDGE, Duke University

Andrew Winston,
Founder, Winston Eco-Strategies

Terry Yogle
President and CEO (retired), World Environment Center

Roger Ballentine
President, Green Strategies Inc. and council facilitator

Marola Avedon
EVP and Chief HR, Marketing and Communications Officer, Trane Technologies

Paul Camuti
EVP and Chief Technology and Strategy Officer, Trane Technologies

Erlo Rankin
VP Environmental, Health and Safety, Trane Technologies

Carrie Ruddy
VP Corporate Communications Trane Technologies

Keith Sultana
SVP Supply Chain and Operational Services, Trane Technologies

W. Scott Tew
VP, Center for Energy Efficiency and Sustainability, Trane Technologies

Source: Scott Tew

Each of these external experts brought new insight to the executives at Trane. The old clogs of Ingersoll Rand were reworked into a new form of competition. The lists of experts is renewed every few years, but they meet with the CEO, the key Executive team, and a few experts in tow. By assembling the external talent to challenge them, Trane has been able to excel in the five areas of its chartered council. While this book does not have the length to get into the details, keep in mind how osmotically open to society, and its climate needs, these six elements became at Trane:

1. Transparency and Reporting

2. Internal Programs and Policies

3. Partnerships and Alliances

4. Product/Process Developments

5. Environmental, Health, and Safety

6. Corporate Strategy and Execution

Do not see these as abstractions. These rigorous measurable categories of self-management established Trane's path forward.

These elements helped them reduce food loss by ten percent, from source of the food to the delivery for consumer purchase—what is known as "cold chain shipping." They also helped them transition faster than their competitors out of high GWP refrigerants, the kind that accelerate the risks and weather disruptions of climate impact.

By 2030, when this book is still young, Trane will have totally transitioned out of high GWP refrigerants, well ahead of global regulations. In addition, they will have brought their approaches to over thirty nations, as they accelerate the cleaner technologies that took out twenty million metric tons of greenhouse magnifiers from their products since 2014.

Such is not the behavior of a robber baron. Instead, this is the behavior of a firm that reinvested into heightened efficiency over half a billion in impactful technological changes. In every corner of business, from Asia to the United States, the technically gifted at Trane enacted equipment that saved greenhouse gas emissions, rather than presumed the endless superabundance and supply of oil.

As oil and industrialism boomed, the late nineteenth and early twentieth centuries became the time of robber barons, who invaded railroads, warehouse contracts, and stocks in pursuit of personal entitlement. For a time, I collected those old stocks of the boom times and framed them into office pictures. They spoke silently, visually, about the power of capital from oil over the dignity of workers. This was fully unintended, but real. The entire notion of capitalists as those holding the means for oil production separated us from family businesses, or firms where we knew our deputies and colleagues. Suddenly, the men in the smoked-filled rooms dominated all.

The Chicago stock exchange, and then the London exchange and the Singapore exchange, boomed with oil and natural gas stocks for nearly a hundred years. In fact, high-tech firms growing in worth more than oil companies only first happened in 2020. Trace stock histories and you'll see that the names Exxon, Chevron, and Saudi Oil dominate stock markets well before you first hear of Apple, Intel, even Tesla. Lloyd was right before he could be right. Now that is insight.

You can say it takes a willingness to step outside the normal petrochemical comfort zone of the last 120 years to become a Trane Technologies. Trane participated with our ongoing leadership workshops, called the Corporate Affiliates programs, for the entire five years of this miracle transformation, so we were privy to changes we cannot detail. Still these general disclosures are now evident in every report and financial disclosure associated with the firm, as a spin-off of the old Ingersoll Rand. Watching such rapid change, we decided to generalize a few new competitive principles from observing Trane in action, calling it "the Sweet Spot of Benefits for Business and Society."

My firm began generalizing competitive principles in our books and management practice, mimicking how Trane, in a larger way, defied normal corporate thinking. We presented it to our clients as aiming for a sweet spot that supplements the needs of both business and society.

This change in principles meant many things to politics and the fate of governments. You can think of the entire award-winning career of Daniel Yergin, leading to his book *The Prize*, as demarcating the more subtle shifts in modern business and society. Today, a new generation of corporates are more comfortable with this dual

SWEET SPOT BENEFITS FOR BUSINESS AND SOCIETY

Business Interests

SUSTAIN-ABILITY SWEET SPOT

Society's Interests
(Including Environment and Social)

BUSINESS RESULTS

- Cut Costs
- Grow Revenue
- Improve Relationships
- Reduce Risk
- Strengthen Brands
- Attract / Retain Talent

$$$

We saw this at Toyota . . .

In our Unilever casework . . .

Energy at giant utilities like NextEra & Iberdrola

Source: Talent, Transformation, and the Triple Bottom Line, Andrew Savitz

competence lens, the bi-focal strengths. They understand that you cannot make advances in HVAC and AI and energy needs without wealth.

Next we examine the role of private and corporate wealth in making this new narrative possible. We do this knowing that some firms, like Tesla and Apple, even outperformed Trane's miraculous increases in stock value; yet I am prepared to argue, that in our age of more transparent disclosures and public expectations on the social contributions of corporations, we have a more stable example of excellence in Trane than we have in Tesla. If you wish to become wealthy from the examples in this book, beware. Stock values are incredibly difficult to sustain.

DINING WITH A BILLIONAIRE'S FATHER

Llyod's book was not actually the first one that would spark my interest in the topic of wealth and corporate responsibility. That happened by chance almost twenty years prior, a good ten years before Trane set up its first World Trends Advisory Council.

Twenty years ago, I had the opportunity to visit "Mr. Gates Senior," as he was then called, at his law firm, Preston Gates Ellis, in Seattle. Mr. Gates Senior was the father of Microsoft founder Bill Gates, one of the world's wealthiest people. I thought our hours would be all business, about the client I was there to discuss with him. Instead, at the end of the meeting, he gave me a book he had written: *Wealth and Our Commonwealth: Why Americans*

Should Tax Accumulated Fortunes. "Let me take an hour to brief you on this book," he said.

I soon came to feel what a privilege it was to sit at his dinner table as he told me about his work. His book was focused on the needs of the wealthy to foster the next estate, and it explained to me the tax logic and social need for this sharing of wealth through the generations.

A key message from his book, one that stuck with me, can be found in his chapter five, "What We Owe Our Society":

> The perspective that society has a claim on individual wealth is reinforced in the teachings of all world religions that we know of. Judaism, Christianity, and Islam all affirm the right of individual ownership and private property, but there are moral limits imposed on absolute private ownership of wealth and property. Each tradition affirms that we are not individuals alone but that we exist in community—a community that makes claims upon us. The notion that "it is all mine" is a violation of these teachings and traditions.

Like a superb attorney, Gates documents with footnotes and citations each of his claims. The book is small, but its notes at the end are rich and its annotated bibliography even richer. Unfortunately, this clear, forceful, honest book was mostly ignored in its time.

But it came back to me that day in the library, decades later, when I saw Lloyd's table of contents. Suddenly, the power of the different times and titles, one from 1894 and another from around the turn of the twenty-first century, stirred more in my emotions than my brain.

Suddenly, the raw and vivid prejudices both books examined came clear to me, like a cold spring snow melt torrent. In one quick synthesis, all my readings since college aligned. These two books rebooted my mind, as it riffled through thousands of great books I read by Freud, Marx, and Darwin, among others, to complete my dissertation and subsequent books. It was what Wallace Stevens, the insurance executive and poet, called "a moment of sudden rightness." I sat in the library chair and realized I would have to write this book.

The narrative of climate competitiveness begins when select firms learn the new language of competition, as Trane did. In this first half of this book, we explore this need for the new narrative by citing progress first started at Trane, and now this new decade actively in pursuit at bp in London. But the goal is larger: helping the reader see how this relates to consumers, the behavior of their family and friends, and what kinds of firms compete in our near future.

In the next passage we now go beyond Trane and generalize some findings from having served five giants now worth more than 400 billion in market cap. This range of five distinct global companies, each representing a completely different market and industrial niche, are significant for our book's themes for several reasons. But the key one is central; If they become as aggressive as Trane in both deed and disclosure to publics than the world will be quite further in the climate goals by 2030.

Most books on climate, like *Carbon Shock* by Mark Schapiro, *Universities on Fire*, by Bryan Alexander, and the impressive books by Bill Gates and Michael Bloomberg touch only the surface of the need to link wealth to climate solutions. These books are a start, but hesitant ones. We offer passages next that go beyond these books of good intentions. In the next half of passages, we reflect the momentum in social history, not only the view of select billionaire authors. In contrast, we present actual changes made by giant manufacturing firms to get on the path of climate competitiveness over the last decade (from 2013 to 2023).

FIVE LEADING FIRMS ACTIVE ON CLIMATE COMPETITIVENESS

A corporation could not become climate competitive without social demand for it. That is the primary fact of social history. There is a set of signals in capital markets and government rulemaking that requires, by implication, such changes in corporate practice. But that is not the full story, it does not capture the full force of change evident in the roll of history itself.

It is critical that you see, from this eighth passage, that the social demand is larger than the legal demands on Trane. It is the same for the five firms we are going to sum up in this passage. Climate competitiveness is about responding with all the tools of capitalism to these larger social demands. That is the key—addressing in act and staff the larger social demands. In responding to social needs, the five leading firms have emerged and matured a set of principles reshaping capitalism and new world companies. At the core of this challenge is corporate responses that matter and last to climate change. **Of course, all firms have the purpose of making money, but those that integrate social trends like all the issues surrounding and integral to climate and energy choices and needs into their actions can expand their margins and compound them. This I've called to clients "the compounding effect of social response capitalism."**

This eighth passage on wealth and climate sums up the competitive principles my firm, and key competitors like EY and the Boston Consulting Group, have witnessed in the last decade. Of the eighty different companies listed in our Corporate Affiliates pages and documents, these five firms paid to join my ongoing leadership workshops—and thereby learn from each other. This gives us a chance to reflect on matters not shared by the EY and the Boston Consulting Group. We focus here on five exceptional leading firms because after years with our companies in the Affiliate leader-to-leader workshops, they then retained us for specific purposes and groups within their firm as "change agents," consultants on a defined mission of change regarding climate, energy, and competition. This passage reflects on the five most effective firms both in stock results, market growth, and leadership training.

We selected these five clients because they all shared a sustained desire to address climate and energy needs of our world. Their actions were sincere, and their executives focused and driven. While I was paid, in confidence, to offer change management and competitive councils within these major firms, I report here general and accurate summaries. I cannot for another ten years write about those specific corporate changes, or the specific personnel in question, without earning the disapproval or lawsuits of my past clients.

I share the general witnessed principles at work in this passage and in our workshops. Over the years, once this book is out, and the world advancing on climate, you can find more competitive principles on **www.wealthand-climatecompetitiveness.net** and information about our changing workshops at **www.ahcgroup.com**.

From 2013 (with the release of my bestseller) to 2023, my firm won several annual retainers, above the Corporate Affiliate memberships, to run and facilitate change management meetings within dozens of global firms. Yet these five stand out as climate innovators but they remain at present less disclosing than Trane.

As a public book writer and as a management consultant, I have been relatively free over the years to reference important work of the Corporate Affiliate companies, major companies that have paid annual membership dues for these leader-to-leader workshops, sometimes for the full decade under summary. More recently, although my writing continues to include anecdotes and examples from these many corporations with whom I've worked, confidentiality and non-disclosure agreements have constrained me and my staff of key executives from citing them by name. The material remains of import, however, so I have shared this passage in this book, if less directly.

Why does this matter?

First off, these summaries serve as concrete indicators that wealth is required to make major change, and that this is shared across five of the eight most climate impactful industries in the world. Firms skating to survive have more trouble getting on the path of climate competitiveness, since they do not have the executive power and the innovative staff to make a difference.

When a well-paid management of change consultant, you are under scrutiny by a team of corporate lawyers and PR agents, even brand executives. Sometimes you are viewed as simply "hired guns," and you must honor total silence. Once outside the mansion, when working in the general neighborhood of policy and market trends, you feel less secure regarding these clients than your workshop attendees, who come to talk and to share. That is the first feature of corporate strategy: those that make it inside these mansions have a sense of security and privacy inside that might not be completely real on the outside. Awareness and experience of this gap between messages in the mansion and outside it changed my understanding of how any giant company—and their thousands of suppliers—can respond to social pressures. It also explains why they make moves to advantage themselves regarding climate vulnerabilities and public infrastructure needs, yet they are not often free to talk about them.

WHAT TO EXPECT WHEN INSIDE THE CORPORATE MANSIONS?

Energy expenditure often determines a large part of the profit margin of major manufacturing firms. This is true whether the firm in question makes flooring, drugs for cancer, carpets, cars, or technological gadgets like cell phones and computers. It is also true if you run a hospital, an aerospace giant, or a competitor of anyone of the mentioned industries above. When this energy spend is discussed in the context of climate responses, it becomes a big sensitive issue, debated by many warring segments within these giant firms. Lobbying weighs in, philanthropy weighs in, executives of all sorts shape the messages on climate. In today's world, climate decisions can prove more sensitive than debates about financial results.

The sensitivity to "the energy annual expenditure numbers" spend is a commonly known variable to any consultant or operating officer within a Fortune 500 or Russell 2000 firm. This is known publicly by giants that announce this public energy cost stress like Dow Chemical. Yet the five firms I am writing about now are too sensitive to energy price volatility globally to weave these explicit numbers in the open breeze of government and public scrutiny. In fact, while they are making inroads on the issues by controlling their risks regarding climate threat and change, they are at best hesitant about drawing attention to how much energy they use to satisfy the cravings of their users. From every meeting I had with these firms, over the last decade, they worked scientifically and diligently through a large list of social needs surrounding climate change and energy innovation.

What we report in this passage is witnessed firsthand; my firm was the retained agent of change in each of these five firms. This means we developed the external expert presentations with their core executive staff, and then we socialized the findings within the leadership teams. I must admit something from the start: we mostly used the same techniques Trane had developed before us. Even before this last decade, these techniques were tried out by visionary executives like Ken Strassner, a Yale attorney who is a senior associate in my firm during this decade, and ran such "external expert" teams when he was senior executive in Atlanta at the global giant Kimberly Clark. It all boils down to the five firm's selection of world trends experts they could trust.

As I now generalize the topics and range of these sessions, note that some of these five firms post stream-lined details of their resultant positions. Look for their web-based carbon-reduction plans in their Corporate Social Responsibility reports, and in their investment ESG briefings. If you do your homework, you can see the results, but the process of getting there is kept confidential in most cases, for good competitive reasons.

Second caveat: not all five do the same process, the same communications, or the same performance indica-tors to do for the investment disclosures on climate. For example, some of the five are extremely secretive regard-ing scope three both in their operations in Europe, North

America, and some in Asia. Others are not. I find that in today's hyper press sensitive world, many CEOs are simply not comfortable with disclosure on climate change. As a result, the general counsels, and, in the net, their executive teams, disfavor disclosure. Another way to say this is they disapprove of disclosure that might reveal a tip on their next directions or plans. This is about staying a few steps ahead of the competition on the path to climate competitiveness.

Nonetheless, all five of the firms in summary have plenty of reports on the web. Moreover, the great majority of the Corporate Affiliates mentioned on our web pages (**www.ahcgroup.com**) do disclose **something of substance about climate** in their CSR or ESG investment reports. Some even sign public certificates on science-based goals like Trane and most big pharma giants. Some create small trade groups to defend before governments their advanced climate positions, ahead of the horde of competitors. Yet what matters more is how these firms brought outside experts to confirm their carbon-neutrality goals. The very dynamics of these outsiders inside is how their business interacts with society on climate and wealth. That became more useful this decade.

This path of the World Trends Expert Council is one of the most promising developments on climate in the last decade. In my experience, this is how these five firms further defeated the popular prejudices slowing up their competition on responding to climate now reshaping big pharma and other industries.

By 2023, we knew some of these firms were already ranked by the Peter Drucker Institute at Stanford as one of the top ten best managed firms in the world. We also knew that some of these firms were being newly run by financial executives, former CFOs becoming CEOs or board members, who were familiar with financial disclosure procedures but were deeply uncomfortable with the more public realm of "climate disclosures." While they knew that these increased disclosures on climate indicates were being advocated by organizations like Michael Bloomberg's Task Force on climate disclosures, they remained hesitant. The thousands of financial institutions that are aligning under Bloomberg's Task Force are perceived as "threatening" to some giant manufacturing firms.

During the birth and maturing of these consulting assignments, we did not how many executives had begun to outsmart many of the prejudices about oil and capitalism that dominate most firms regarding private wealth, corporate responsibility, and the management of social change. In this way, the five leading firms were rapid followers of Trane. In retrospect, that is the real amazing ingredient of these five noted firms—their leaders, to the individual, were more than financial and science-based wizards from the start. (Another way to say this: you do not get hired to come inside a corporate mansion by dinosaur firms.) From the general counsel to the top manufacturing facilities executives, each leader within these five leaders responded to society and its needs, not only to the usual market signals.

Once inside the mansion, you hear a good deal not in the books or the disclosures. These were the statements by key executives about their worldview and sustaining culture. Often there were fascinating discussions about how the best science could no longer be "insular" to corporate settings, or "reserved" for the rich. Some of the five actively pursued "clusters of corporate partners" that enabled them to transcend inherited biases within their industry type, joining groups like the Chief Executive for Corporate Purpose to widen their views. Others of the five noted that resilience in society had become a "shared problem for all large businesses." They consistently noted that if their firms were to thrive "in this new world" (some even cited my book *New World Companies* here) they would have to continue to observe governments as key clients. As top executives they noted in both private and investment calls that they needed to perform in a manner that was more focused on climate, energy, and innovation. What all five shared was this emphasis of remaining on the path to climate competitiveness.

All of this was focused on what "the five" often called "carbon neutral" strategies and plans. Please see again our opening summary of these definitions in passage 1. If you want more detail on definitions now, please go to the annotated bibliography at the end by the attorney Ira Feldman. This bibliography on the nuance and citations of this still rapidly emerging field of expertise can help you see the range of concerns and issues before us when we look at both wealth and climate at once.

Were there repeatable rules or patterns by which these firms brought the outside experts inside the mansions? Well, all five shared competitive principles once inside the mansion, but not outside. Some appointed only their internal staff on these councils. Some appointed only five external experts, some appointed twenty external experts. And a few did a hybrid, like Trane, joining internal top executives on the same council with external experts. It is not an exact science this path to climate competitiveness. And for me, my past training as a social historian helped me be flexible enough to frame the discussions depending on the culture and worldview of the firm. I do this to explain how the thinking of Freud, Marx, and Darwin, plus the mounting pressures of social movements, played a key role in enabling these changes in the modern corporation.

None of this could have happened without impressive wealth to explore, investigate, and respond to external inputs. That is a major takeaway in watching and facilitating how these five firms achieved competitive advantages through its stepping onto the path of climate competitiveness. Over the last decade, each of the five firms I am generalizing about were profitable. Some not as profitable as Trane, and none more profitable in stock dynamics than Trane, but some quite profitable in terms of the Fortune 500, the Russell 2000. These were darling firms in the eyes of investment retirement funds like TIAA-CREF, or the universal stock owners like retirement funds and pooled asset firms. They had momentum, value, paths of improvements and social response in their reports.

WHAT IS CLIMATE COMPETITIVENESS?

We will start with three main points, then offer the insight to some of the expert outsiders, and then come back and answer this question with three additional summary points further defining climate competitiveness.

What stunned me the most about these five leading firms was their love and respect of science. As for Trane, bp and the others it is how they made decisions on climate, not by reading the policy tea leaves or the public affairs and marketing reports. They brought the outside world of experts inside their corporate mansion with greater consistency and response than their benchmarked peers and competitors. I took away from this experience at a few lessons that could be transferred to all competitive firms, more than 5000 of them worthy stocks.

1. Climate competitiveness is a comprehensive corporate response to a range of issues surrounding business and society. It is larger than the kinds of corporate strategy seminars you hear at the best business schools. Climate competitiveness involves the blending of private scientific and market knowledge, both corporate culture and corporate ambitions, years ahead of anticipated carbon taxes and regulatory demand. We need enough wealth in the system of corporations to allow such innovation.

2. Climate competitiveness involves a responsible, steady, resolve-based focus on lessons derived from human behavior and social movements. In other words, when it works best, climate competitiveness is a corporate response to social needs.

3. None of this work represents the normal prejudice that speculative capitalists are birds of prey, swooping over markets to exploit and kill. Instead, this chapter explores how it took one hundred years of social thinking and social movements to bring these five firms into their current positions on the climate crisis as real and concerning future competitive advantage. What is true, instead, is that this kind of work takes panic and resolve, the two forward-looking features of the human psyche. Often the firm using the world trends experts to tie their numbers and strategy to something that will be compounded "in the near future" (next 60 months, usually) by social expectations and shifts in markets. These five complex firms operate very much like Unilever, Trane, and bp when they compete for energy resources and address climate matters. I have written before in detail about Unilever, CAT, Toyota and others in this vein. Yet the five leading firms have taken their competitive strategies beyond even CAT and Toyota on climate further into serious changes in energy usage, building science, competitive differentiation, manufacturing efficiency, but seldom public climate politics. You will note the great firms always want "a few good

options" to deliver their optimal corporate strategy. Unilever, being a consumer giant in over 170 nations, is a mammoth message machine on climate competitiveness but not one of the five now summarized.

4. The bottom line remains this: Each of the five firms proved themselves a reliable **business in society, not a business beside society**. That is required before you can see climate competitiveness at work.

You might ask, then, how does one start at a firm, once invited inside the mansion?

All great firms study their competition, benchmark their positions (per regional market and sometimes particular national markets) and promises, and then attempt to exceed them. We advised each of the five firms on this by first spending sometimes just a month, sometimes for as long as a year before bringing in the full council. In short, here you are studying their climate competitiveness capabilities and announcements of their closest competitors. This is why I always went to key researchers from MIT, Cornell, Yale, Carnegie Mellon and Tufts to supplement the retired executives on my staff. There was basic research to do at the start of the process.

A PERSONAL ASIDE

This kind of work fell my firm's way because my book *Doing More with Less: The New Way of Winning* was being noticed, both in sales and by top executives at the five firms. (For those in need of the details, you can now consult *Doing More with One Life: A Writer's Journey through the Past, Present, and Future*, a memoir out this Fall of 2023.) Often, I was asked to apply for this kind of work. It is often not won by public bidding. I felt the first inquiry came from executives seeing me on BBC or Wall Street TV, not necessarily from any one at top of a firm first reading the book. That came later upon hire, where staff wrote synoptic slides about my books. I saw these at meetings, brilliant summaries of the books, for the top executives to scan.

By the end of the books' best-selling seasons in 2015, I was scanning the globe to provide these five firms introductions to many of the world's leading experts, from investment houses to other giant firms like Lockheed Martin. In a few rare cases, we even brought in experts from Switzerland, Australia's Royal Society (200 years old), and a few from Asia. This introduction of leaders to leaders was a natural off-shoot of my workshops, done twice a year for decades by this time. While the workshops are mostly North American executives, this list of 100 top world trends experts is truly global.

Most of these meetings occurred in "executive" English. Some of these selected executives knew continental thinking either as graduate students in Europe or as general readers of greats like Freud and Darwin. At private meals during long workdays, I was shocked that some even talked with me about Karl Marx's texts and claims. They always liked my jokes about these nineteenth-century great writers. The executives hosting these outsiders were quite civil and rehearsed in dinner chat.

Most of the time we would appoint, on average, across the five firms, seven leaders for three years. It was rare for these assignments to last a year, and some lasted five years, but the average was three years of duration, and about seven outsiders. These included leaders from my Corporate Affiliates workshops. That is the key. The firms first saw the world trends leaders in our private sanctuary twice a year.

THE ROLE OF BENCHMARKING IN CORPORATE CHANGE WORK

All great firms study their competition. They "benchmark" their competitor's positioning and promises, and then attempt to exceed them. We provide two short examples from the large pharma firm Johnson & Johnson. We never served Johnson & Johnson directly (although I was sent to Wall Street to assess the range of their CEO's speech and interactions before CECP once). One client dove deep into Johnson & Johnson and Exxon Mobil because this client had curiosity about their marketing claims on climate promises and positions. We also always gave our clients examples of smaller innovators like you see below in the case of Novartis. I never worked at Novartis, although one member of my research team had.

We advised each of our five leading clients on "their positions relative to the benchmarking reports," which of course are confidential, often submitted only to the

General Counsel and the Corporate Secretary. You know it is sensitive when these studies go first to these folks rather than first to your usual client manager of the project. The point being we had a boxful of first-hand interviews and data on many competitors, who sometimes spoke at our workshops in PowerPoint sets, as we facilitated the competitive change at the client home/mansion. That meant we had expertise and research in five of the dominant ten big greenhouse-emitting industries, constituting the bulk of the impact. **Please also note that great firms often ask for benchmarking outside of their direct industry type.** The modern giant firms often retain three "competing" advisory groups like EY and Boston Consulting Group, at different levels of the organization. These groups are much larger than my boutique firm. This enables them to afford expert researchers in all ten of the major industries contributing to the climate crisis. My books gave me a leg up on early hires in this space, but over time, I lost more and more to EY and Boston Consulting Group as they built up their global capabilities and staff.

Nonetheless, these five leading giants did engage us many times for benchmarking services. Here are two summary examples among hundreds we provided between the five leading clients in the last decade, always up to the date of submission of the work.

Some great firms work hard to differentiate their offerings in a social context, for competitive advantage. Look to my cases on Shaw Industries, HP, Toyota and

J&J AND BIOGEN COMMITMENTS

- Sourcing 100% of electricity needs from renewable sources by 2025

- Achieving carbon neutrality in operations by 2030
    - Energy efficiency effort while evaluating alternative fuel sources, fleet vehicle choices and refrigerants towards zero emissions

- Reducing upstream carbon footprint by 20% by 2030
    - Launch new work streams in carbon intensive procurement categories including logistics, chemicals, external manufacturing and packaging, among others

Biogen

- Launched HealthyClimate, HealthyLives—$250M, 20-year initiative

- Become fossil fuel free—to go beyond carbon neutrality by eliminating emissions by 2040

- Collaborating with global leaders, including MIT and the Harvard T. H. Chan School of Public Health, to use data science and predictive analytics to drive strategies to mitigate environmental and health impacts from climate change as well as influence policy and improve health outcomes, particularly for the world's most vulnerable populations

Source: Biogen Inc. Sept. 14, 2020

NOVARTIS SUSTAINA-BILITY EFFORTS & GOALS

NEXT GENERATION GOALS:
- Carbon neutrality in own operations
- 50% carbon emissions reduction across value chain
- Water neutrality
- Plastic neutrality
- Pushing hard into renewables
    - Virtual PPA—Wind Farm, TX—eliminating carbon footprint in US and Canada for all electricity

Social Impact = 30g400% roi in local communities

SUPPLY CHAIN:
- Partnership with MIT—identify 4 key risk factors of climate change at 70 global sites

- Help remove barriers and ensure access to suppliers (increased technology, renewable energy, offset programs)

Environmental targets / objectives are a part of the personal objective of senior leaders. Provide information / resources to associates.

LOOKING AHEAD...
- How technology will scale

- Power of digital technologies to track and predict impact on environment; track carbon footprint in real time and how their actions being taken are impacting their footprint

- Go beyond operations and across the value chain

Unilever in prior books as early proof of how firms are competing for social context now. Yet in the case of our five leading examples in the last decade, they often started with aggressive benchmarking of their direct and indirect competitors for advantage regarding the scientific and general executives needs of greenhouse gas emissions reductions. In short, these five went further than my prior case studies in books from 2005 to 2022.

By the end of 2023, I was scanning the globe to provide data bio sheets of about a hundred of the world's leading experts, from investment houses to other giant firms like Lockheed Martin, to Board members and doctors and independent lawyers. The five firms tended to select executives, not lawyers or doctors, in most cases. Yet one doctor, who founded a Medical Consortium on Climate and Public Health, was selected by three of the five leading firms. The final decision was often made by committee before me, in live meetings (or during Covid live Zooms) with key corporate folks. Sometimes I offered candidates who had no chance of being selected: one investment head from Switzerland and some even from major hospitals were not selected. One great doctor on medical bias was not selected by any of the five, I believe, because of her dyed pink hair and "radical" politics about social justice.

Here is the lesson to take at this point in our book about wealth and climate.

There is a wealth of expertise on climate innovation out there, both the investment community and with those with operational expertise in climate. The second lesson, in looking over the differences of the resumes of our 100 world trends experts: There are as many world experts as there are company types. That is why when establishing an advisory council on impact, you need to work with the firm to select the right mix of agents of change for their worldview and culture. You need to have, in short, access to a hundred "critical friends" of impact who are successful in these elements of change management—as a firm will select on average only five to seven leaders.

RELATING THE COUNCIL TO THE LARGER CONCERNS OF EACH OF THE FIVE GIANT FIRMS

There are a few deeper lessons to share beyond the eight listed in this passage.

You need to remain humble in designing these teams, as they are only outsiders after all. They have no executive decision-making authority within the host corporate mansion, even though they may be running their own organizations with hundreds of staff. We went into each selection process of our world trends experts knowing that these five leading firms had mature risk management teams. Thus, both risk profiles (kept private) and regional risks were paramount in World Trend Expert final selections, I found.

Before my internal team of experts accepted the "change assignments" we knew already each of the five hiring firms had discerned climate risks scientifically.

But we also knew they reached out to us because they needed to scan history, with its entrenched prejudices about corporate behavior, to make and support more reliable internal decisions. Neither of these processes—the governance system and the risk management process—were directly disclosed to our Council experts. In other words, all five keep you somewhat in the dark, forgetting how much information is out there already about their performances. However, we were aware that you could not make any of the five leading firms, or any of the thousands of leaders in our workshops, truly modern without first having them open to understanding social expectations. You might at this point ask: how did I prepare myself to get inside such complex organizations?

You might now ask: How do you cope with so much uncertainty, and in a sense, working in the dark?

MY SILENT PARTNERS AT THE FIVE LEADING FIRMS: FREUD, HENRY DAVID THOREAU, AND DARWIN

Most of my work is illuminated by social history. I got inside as a social trends expert, who happens to know about company behaviors. Over the first decades of my firm, my employers were not these five giants. We were hired by smaller organizations with big ambitions. I had to experience work with nearly a third of the fortune 500 by the start of this last decade (2013 to 2023), before these multi-year complex climate-related assignments came to us. Often, we did not apply for this kind of work, but the firm came to us because of our sanctuary of workshops. They could see from the books that we had benchmarking research skills. They could see from the twice-a-year workshops involving a hundred executives across the year that we were trusted by hundreds of executives from many different industries.

This is why all five of the giants had us look at my friend Frank Loy's role at Exxon Mobil's corporate citizenship committee. Let me be clear, bp never needed this information. I present more on bp later for different reasons. Our corporate affiliate bp knew about ExxonMobil. It was the other Corporate Affiliates wanting to see how a big oil firm under climate pressure "staffed up" to deal with the new world. I had written a book about Frank Loy and a former CEO of bp Steve Percy once, and so the firms knew I could gain some insight into the pressures felt at Exxon regarding climate change. All five of the leading firms were interested in the fate of ExxonMobil regarding climate politics and civil pressures on climate. They also knew from www.ahcgroup.com that we had already served firms like Suncor Energy and Hess for years with select big oil former executives on my team. Thus, each of the five had us examine the external committees at many large firms from ExxonMobil, bp and Hess to key financial institutions like Blackrock, Goldman, and the progressives like Calvert and Trillium. This was another way to bring trends in society back into the firm, without too much bias and prejudice. These benchmarking findings helped each firm "get out of the box" of their own prejudices, culture, and worldview, in a sense.

THE TAKE AWAYS ON WEALTH AND CLIMATE

We found in the history of our workshops, especially these last ten years (2013 to 2023) several key attributes that mattered on the path to climate competitiveness:

1. The corporate mission must be aligned with global trends, not simply their existing five-year product development strategy. That is a compelling and disabling limit in how corporate strategy is taught to old world executives today, even at the great business schools like Manchester England, INSEAD, Harvard Business and Stanford, places I've been hired to visit on my books. Old world strategy could reside mostly in financial literacy and legal precedent. But this new kind of world dealt more with the intersection of global megatrends and climate science, as well as national and regional needs about floods, asset protection, and severe weather on workers. That is what makes these World Trend Expert Councils so modern and insightful.

2. The Council results on scope one and scope two emissions must maximize positive returns to customers and their surrounding communities. Social response capitalism responds to global trends in legislation, the press, and the investment community. It remains a vital part of the present, and future, of major corporations. Social

response capitalism provides an alert firm the license to operate in society and the investment community, and it ensures that these leading firms maintain those capacities in the future. That is the basis of investment, not just credit worthiness.

3. We often, at the five, used a map to remind ourselves of their global research and manufacturing scope. The map was often (three of the five cases) presented to us by their global head of facilities at the time. In this way, we stayed close to "actual" and "operational" capitalist needs of the firm. Social response firms— if truly great—do not fall prey to vague notions of corporate responsibility. This requires attention to talent pools, as demonstrated already by Trane, and to focus on social trends more lasting than temporary market perturbations. I wrote about this in the Unilever case in my book *A New Way to Wealth*, for example, as recently as 2022. Unilever is famous for looking beyond quarterly financial reports in its brand and world market dominance. Again, Unilever is not one of the five under summary.

4. We knew, from our study of social movements, that each of the five leading clients, needed to improve partnerships at major stakeholder institutions— Universities to think tanks—across the world, and that it had to strengthen their brand and reputation for improved transparency. This is historically still true for most of our workshop firms, and that is why they keep

coming back to refine their prospects. This is how the great firms emerge from the lesser ones in their search to doing more with less, and to bend the curve on global warming. Trane was right at the right moment: as the world wanted to secure more healthy food, water, Covid vaccinations and medicines. The other five had similar but not as many sweet spots.

5. Finally, in each of the five leading firms we are generalizing these new century trends stood out: their core leaders share the same financial discipline to protecting and enhancing their portfolio returns. Yet each was sensitive to response to rapidly increasing climate pressures. In other words, they are expert at financial literacy but they go beyond it in affording to address social needs in trends and actions.

By the end of each assignment inside a corporate mansion, we do not leave totally successful. You do not win all your points. When you work for an intelligent set of strong executives, you learn to get to essences quickly. This is what made our work so exciting through the decades. But how did my training allow this kind of big picture change work?

The key take away from this case is this: My silent partners in many of my consulting assignments have been the medical findings of Freud (as modernized by neuroscience and the cognitive sciences), the sense of competition for resources in Darwin (as modernized by modern scientific studies of people and cultures in change), and an appreciation of the power in Henry David Thoreau, as a signal of things to come in social expectations about privacy, peace of mind, and human creativity. These giants helped us advance our appreciation of both business and society. Some of our best Corporate Affiliates were large extractive industries like mining giants, who build things. Who would have guessed their executives were so well read?

Let's start with Thoreau. I have come to conclude, after forty years of management practice, that it takes Thoreau's civic tone of mind to become climate competitive. Here are a few Thoreau quotes from my travelling notebook that I used again and again in facilitation practice:

1. "Rather than love, than money, than fame, give me truth."

2. "Disobedience is the true foundation of liberty. The obedient must be slaves."

3. "As if you could kill time without injuring eternity."

4. "Our truest life is when we are in our dreams awake."

5. "How vain it is to sit down to write when you have not stood up to live."

6. "Read the best books first, or you may not have a chance to read them at all."

7. "Wealth is the ability to fully experience life."

8. "True friendship can afford true knowledge. It does not depend on darkness and ignorance."

9. "A man is rich in proportion to the number of things he can afford to let alone."

10. "Every generation laughs at the old fashions, but religiously follows the new."

Very few of the leaders in my workshops could laugh at themselves, like Thoreau laughed explicitly at the old-fashioned robber baron habits—as they stretched and reshaped new, more socially responsive aspirations. Yet perhaps this "stiffness" to self-criticism comes with the solemnity of being a major decision maker at major global firms.

Yet the executives that excelled at the featured five firms could at times laugh at themselves. They were open inside their corporate mansions. They are not promoted if they are stray birds of prey. This was not always true, but it was in general truth. They are promoted for bringing value to society at large and to the firm's bottom line. In other words, the great firms have leaders that create near future value, not just existing margins. The executives constitute a mansion of expert talent that demonstrates how a business is meant to answer social and public health needs, including the new needs of health created by the climate crisis.

I call these new century executives ready for this century of corporate and climate change. (See my book *New World Companies: The Future of Capitalism* for a denser set of details about CAT, Toyota, and Flex if you want more case work.) They must, again, fit these dominant company cultures yet still align with the larger social mission of bringing greater health and wellness across the globe.

And here is the fun part of the change work. I can say from talking with these executives at dinners—after a long day—**they have already read the important books first,** as Thoreau advised. Many of my best clients have proven themselves learning machines. An example is Steve Percy and Frank Loy (again see my biographies on these two exceptional leaders). They know the works of Sigmund Freud, his updating, as well as the works of Charles Darwin. Being both lawyers and executives, they are also bright and interested in a range of people and things. My five past clients, overall, are staffed at the top by intelligent social engineers who might also be informed global MBAs with a broad comprehensive sense of people, staff, and their changing attitudes on consumption, climate, and work style. They know the past greats, and they know what is changing in society. It is this dual business and society view that allows the advances in climate competitiveness. In this way, they are applied humanists as well as gifted leaders in terms of proportion, modern corporate diagnostics, and science.

Over these last ten years of day-to-day practice, it was remarkable to see how efficiently workshop attendees (now consisting of over 1000 different people in 40 years) could afford to let idle peripheral things alone, then immediately focus on what was rich and of social use before them. They were seldom distracted like our public by Trump, the market swings, or temporary trends. You might call this "disciplined strategic focus," but it also relies on seasoned "socially alert" executives. They had insights both into the power of wealth creation, and the obligations it brought to them in society. This ability to sustain and to shift focus is far more mature in these workshop executives than I saw in training graduates and the average executive MBA at RPI for a decade at the end of last century.

I apologize to my readers for the length of passage eight. Writing about five large secretive firms, about climate and wealth, and the experts they came to trust, is not available in a few sentences, as in the six shorter passages of this book. But I hope you see how it all adds up at the end.

THERE IS A PARADOX
IN ADVANCING HISTORY

Every human is the product of their culture and their history, both family history and general social trends. I learned about these in college, during my dissertation research on the works of Freud, Charles Darwin, and Marx. I then taught these classics in my classes as a young professor for ten years.

The work of Henry David Thoreau embodies peak moments in the nineteenth century. There are so many great writers in the nineteenth century—Sigmund Freud on the frontiers of the mind, Darwin on the competition within nature, and Marx on the struggles within social economic markets. Yet Thoreau wrote about wealth and the commons with a set of lasting passages, where you could see into the twentieth century and beyond. I found such passages also in the work of other great nineteenth-century writers like Freud and Darwin. They reached into the needs of the new century with their work insights based on practice and observation.

In recalling the great works of Henry David Thoreau, we see how he led to social movements on civil rights, Black Lives Matter, social inclusion, and the dramatic advantages of diversity on design and results. Think of this as proactive social history. These are parallel, if not congruent, with many of the things executives consider emerging issues in business and society during our discussions.

I believe there is nothing more important for the rest of this century than to get the balance right between social movements and a robust marketplace, both global and swift.

What Henry David Thoreau means for the commonwealth, and what he saw in the wealthy in corporations and the power elite, matters not only for our present day but for our near future, and for the global society that surrounds us. He was a quintessentially Bostonian American, whose insights into human nature and the needs of the commons has had a tidal impact on the full world.

My historic point is clear: Thoreau is recommending that all intelligent citizens, with an informed sense of civics and history, be willing to be voices and actors of civil disobedience—agents of positive change without violence. The executives I served embodied these civic principles, not just their corporate imperatives. This underlines another higher fact: once they get on the path of climate competitiveness, select public parties and investors notice the improvements, and award the firm greater stock value.

Once you feel the present and perennial power in Thoreau, you realize your flight in life will be larger and further than mere speculative capitalism. You move from competitors for self-advancement to persons of social value. You allow the company to compete at a higher social level.

In re-reading the history of this great text with today's social movements in mind, you can see that it is wrong to assume what you earn will depend on what you learn; you can make it if you try. That dream of the endless frontier of resource-intensive prospects for all peoples has been proven wrong.

While devoting passages to self-determination and self-reliance, Thoreau's work is fundamentally about finding social value in one's life by doing social good. What Emerson called philosophically in poetic prose "self-reliance," Thoreau embodied in prose that made people act, not think. That is the difference. Social movements prove, to me and to many, that it is wrong to assume that if someone fails it is a problem of self-motivation. If we assume that capitalists come in many forms, from eagles and hawks to speculative self-aggrandizing aggressors (they are now called hedge fund managers), then we are getting ready now to ask deeper questions. In order to thrive in our time of carbon and climate constraints, we must realign regarding human flourishing and what enables the social values in a firm. By getting back to Walden Pond, Thoreau suggests this takes a protest song.

It would be accurate to say that what today we call "good trouble," Thoreau called "civil disobedience." And of course, for Thoreau this worldview and life of actions was a form of thriving outside the petrochemical treadmill of over-industrialization. Thoreau was not against business; instead, his constructive work was about improving the balance of business and society.

THE CREATIVE FORCE IN SOCIAL MOVEMENTS

There are two primary captivating metaphors in the works of Thoreau that fill the lungs of youth through the ages:

1. The first presents the dominant culture as a machine, where an informed minority has the dignified ability to stick their shoes in the machine to stop it. By World War II, some social critiques called this machine the "industrial war machine complex." For Thoreau, and for most of the world, the apt metaphor is a machine, any machine, where the operator is free/capable to alter its operations.

2. The second metaphor, more hidden yet persistent in cultures, presents capitalists as birds of prey. In my prior books, I've referred to these types of capitalists as speculative capitalists. See my book *World Inc.*, for example.

Many at bp, and Trane, and the five unnamed giants are now devoted to solutions on climate. They embody shifts you will see throughout this book in the general direction that the elephant of policy and science marches in society. And where that elephant marches, technologies and markets change and grow for the better in the eyes of society.

This proclivity for corporate and civil action becomes the final resting place and wisdom in the essay "Civil Disobedience," as it now does for our generation.

We next tackle the harder case of transforming an oil giant, in the form of bp from London. We can only do this by jumping ahead to an image of Robin Hood. For you cannot change an oil giant without changing its aim.

THE FABULOUS BIRTH OF THE LEISURE CLASS CAPITALISM

The wealth of this world surrounds.

Yet excessive wealth exhausts our resources and our lives. That much has been displayed by the environmental and sustainability movements since the 1970s. The world needs a new narrative on private wealth, corporate purpose, and future solutions on climate challenges.

Climate competitiveness is about balancing the cash flow needs of innovation with the arts of competitive frugality. Individuals need enough excess in their lives to be creative and to know their roles in the expanding globalized world. The great value-based corporates need enough excess in their firms to afford the major innovations found in an oil and gas giant like bp.

You can see this social truth in thinking about a set of these following touchstones in popular social history. As I list them, think of how they appealed for both market results and social results, and while they transpired during a time of leisure, they also were of social value, commemorating universal attributes of the seasons after the long dark days of winter:

1. E. B. White's classic of 1952, *Charlotte's Web*, spoke with great lasting care about humor, friendship, and children's wisdom.

2. Aaron Copland's musical composition *Appalachian Spring*, premiered in 1944, but came to seem an apt soundtrack for all springs.

3. T. S. Eliot, in his iconic 1921 poem, notes in the *Waste Land* that "April is the cruelest month," with its hint of spring after the darkened aftermath of World War I.

4. Walt Whitman's "When Lilacs Last in the Dooryard Bloomed" became a memorable ode to spring not just a commemorative piece on the death of Abe Lincoln in 1865.

5. Claude Monet's *Water Lilies* became a vibrant emblem of spring as well, that helped define what was universal in impressionism. They were simply fun to look at.

I offer these five cultural touchstones to remind us that we all have a sense of social history, its high points, and its lasting values.

Yet we, as general citizens of this consumptive world, cannot fully understand social response firms until we understand how to overcome the past mistakes of the leisure class, and then embrace the future solutions of energy innovation. You can think of this idea of social response capitalism as being about the re-enchantment of the better elements of capitalism as it competes on price, quality, talent, and social needs. That is what enables us to avoid the knuckleheads of waste and get on the path of climate competitiveness.

With that said, you may ask: But can we transfer big oil itself in this time of climate challenges?

WHY BP IS TANSFORMING WITH CONSEQUENCES TO MANY

In this passage, we explore the complex case of bp since Bernard Looney became CEO in December of 2020. Of all firms in the market, big oil suffers some of the most severe popular prejudices due to their legacy of past mistakes. Yet, even today, few know of their quest to create future solutions of significant social value.

In short, we need to know how corporate and private wealth answer our new needs for climate competitiveness.

In this chapter we will explore the risks and benefits of the leisure class relative to a new kind of oil company, the transformed energy company bp run by Bernard Looney. While I have not met him in person, I've seen him perform in front of his EVPs, his staff, and the investment company several dozen times. Following is a personal

bp

THE VISION OF BERNARD LOONEY

bp

"We believe our new strategy provides a comprehensive and coherent approach to turn our net zero ambition into action. This coming decade is critical for the world in the fight against climate change, and to drive the necessary change in global energy systems will require action from everyone."

"So, in the years ahead, bp is going to significantly scale up our low-carbon energy business and **transform our mobility and convenience offers.** We will focus, and reduce, our oil, gas and refining portfolio. And, as we drive down emissions on our route to net zero, we are committed to **continuing to deliver longterm value for all stakeholders.**"

—BERNARD LOONEY, CEO bp

- Note transform **for mobility**

- Transform "**convenience**" (social markets value)

- Long-term value proposition (**compounding** 6-8)

MANTRA THAN MATTERS TO INVESTORS:
Decarbonization | Delivery | Decentralization | Digitalization

account of what makes this professional an exemplar case of transformation, the voice of a CEO in change.

ALONG THE WAY AVOID WASTE AND KNUCKLEHEADS

What contrasts CEO Bernard Looney from former big oil CEOs is his modesty, plus his focus on frugality and select social and business alliances. That is the tale of the new bp, which after one hundred years of world-roaming went through a rebranding from BP, the bold British Petroleum, to bp.

Look at how Looney personally relies on a social vision to achieve his transformative set of aims. When you look at these aims think through how the relationship between the firm and its social setting is osmotic, semipermeable, not isolated.

As I got to know many of the dozen key executive vice presidents that cluster around Looney, I concluded that this original draft of the aims comes from Looney's hands. Of course, other leaders and the board helped sharpen his take on clean cities or reducing methane, but overall, this culture is his. He took over a very British global empire and matured it for this world of climate demand. He added a sense of humility and social purpose up front.

This stands in stark contrast to how we've become used to viewing oil companies and modern wealth. It's important to examine this contrast here. The prevailing and preceding myths about companies as birds of prey,

AIMING FOR ZERO

Five aims to become
a net zero company

Five aims to help the
world meet net zero

1 Net Zero
Operations

6 Clean Cities

2 Net Zero
Oil & Gas

7 Transparency
Leader

3 Halving
Intensity

8 Aligning
Associations

4 Reducing
Methane

9 Incentivizing
Employees

5 More $ For
New Energies

10 Advocating

Remember to attach each of these aims to an
EVP's objective and compensation

about oil destroying a sense of social responsibility, are all transformed in these larger aims by bp.

Examine, patiently, Looney's list of big bold changes:

Align associations, so he puts money into positive change.

Incentivize employees.

Have more money for new energy

Reduce methane

Have energy intensity in operations

Support clean cities

Be a transparency leader, etc.

Each topic for EVP examination at bp has a consistent consumer facing this world of change. We each have to choose a flight path of consumption for our family, friends, and firms. Within bp, I found a larger shareable story about the arts of competitive change and frugality amongst great wealth and transformation. The new narrative goes something like this:

In all birds of prey, molting is natural. In all civilizations, I've found that capital accumulation leads to waste and "some fluff." For visual convenience, let's call that fluff the "molting" of the capitalist. Today we need new narratives that reflect on this kind of molting, as opposed to the power displays of kings and queens and those self-appointed to rule in politics.

I remember refusing a second-year lucrative engagement with a young CEO (his father was wealthy and famous and flamboyantly reserved). This young, entitled CEO moved his primary team to expensive Manhattan headquarters, so he could boat around each weekend off Long Island. As I worked for him and got him some stable cash and contracts, he extended each weekend longer—from two days galivanting in the Hamptons, to three days around the coast, to full four-day escapades with friends from prep school and college.

I discovered that he had nothing to do with the hands-on of a start-up business. He hired a contractor with his dad's money to do that. This hands-off ap-proach seldom works in discovering a path of climate competitiveness.

When he told me about the joy of destroying three motor engines by hitting his boat on a rock going twenty-five miles an hour, I said I had had enough, and resigned with my key lawyer on the assignment.

I submitted my final report to the CEO and his team that moving to Manhattan was a waste for every square inch. His CFO and friendly board members understood what we advised. A rural and better HQ would allow all of them to work in more frugal ways. At the end of the report, against the will of my attorney in house, I stated that I and my firm would not work for him while he com-mitted so much destructive wastefulness.

I am not sure he got it. He was more concerned about dramatic excess than practical business. That CEO did not know what a real pragmatic frugal business strategy must entail these days. We parted ways, and in time, his firm failed, as I sailed forward.

Contrast this with Looney, who led others in staff reductions in the oil patch when he first joined bp. By focusing on each technical staff member's agility, commercial instincts, and sense of sustainability, he shocked some entrenched petroleum engineers into discomfort and radical change. Many left, many more were fired. A dozen EVPs became eleven, and some excess was reduced.

ENOUGH, BUT NOT EXCESSIVE WASTE

As Tom Wolfe dramatizes throughout his novel *Bonfire of the Vanities*, modern wealth is flamboyant. Wolfe was a master at exposing American greed, largess, and stupidities.

He invited me to join his Lotos Club in Manhattan the year he noticed my *New York Times* bestseller. Wolfe felt *Doing More with Less* was a "title for the rest of this century," when we need to be reminded how small the world actually has become. It was always fun talking with him about excess, seen by him as special and mesmerizing in America. He is the one that made me advance past the theories of Thorstein Veblen, and instead, fly over the plumage and molting of the leisure class.

The evidence of the molting is highly visible in the young. Wolfe said it is always fun to notice excess in the young as they molted into the arrogance of the teen years; before it sheds in college and in the "afterlife," as he called it.

Wealth of this world surrounds us, and some of its financial forms are flamboyant. But the issue is how to have just enough excess, not excessive excess.

It is the same with the food requirements of the birds of prey, and the resource requirements of all capitalists. You have the basic minimum required in a meal; then you have an additional increment that must be reserved in cold weather or bad down markets. There will always be some wasted portion of the kills, and while great birds of prey scanning the Patagonia or the remote deserts have less than the norm, there is always a "waste of the kill." It is a matter of degree.

Speculative capitalists allow a larger waste than socially responsible capitalists. I can measure that in staff, title, function, and results now.

Remember this in your career. Speculative capitalists add excessive costs and waste—a bad kind of reserve. Instead, learn your basic minimum to sustain. Only you can discern the actual amount needed to obtain basic needs. All solid competitors must be these sleeker birds of prey. The difference between survival as a capitalist, and common failure, is in the waste.

THE GOLDEN EAGLES OF CAPITALISM

Capitalism today, and in the future, is not only about the means of production on a massive scale. Instead, it is about creativity of social value. It is about aligning money, people, and rules.

It is easy for most of us to think of capitalists, when celebrated, flying through life like a golden eagle. Mobility allows the golden eagle to soar effortlessly over miles to secure its favorite prey. It may be the same for certain venture capitalists too. Some capitalists have no sense of social needs. Others capitalize on social needs, like the inventors of the handheld, hybrid cars, and the new generation of rooftop solar panels.

I've studied the modern capitalist long enough to notice how the range of the majority perceive their range and their use of resources. The informing prejudice is that the people lump all companies and their leaders into the same pot, calling them all birds of prey.

I now ask you to avoid being distracted by the molting in youth. I ask you to suspend your biases about old and new wealth. Please note how a giant oil firm needs cash to manage a rapid transition to a more climate friendly and cleaner future. The passages here identify the wasteful. Avoid the fluff, the molting, and side-step the knuckleheads who might trip you up.

Examining bp in this context of excess, this chapter asks you to dig deeper to compose your own protest song based on competition and frugality. As explored through the prior chapters, this bp case helps you cultivate a sense of civil disobedience, to feel a part of the social movements rather than a reactionary force against the leisure classes. Like Henry David Thoreau before him, Looney was a rebel in the oil patch, disrupting other giants to action (like France's Total, and Shell Oil). Perhaps a more accurate rendition of history is to note that all these giants got a sense of the same changes and challenges before them.

That is the point to keep in mind as we contemplate how the large global oil and gas giant BP transformed itself in the first decades of this new century, and by 2023, into a firm fostering clean energy, the marketing of other people's cleaner fuels, and the global electrification of the automobile. Many commentators claim this humbling happened because of the large Gulf oil spill; yet it came down to leadership over events.

WHAT IS SOCIAL RESPONSE CAPITALISM

We can now return to our opening claims about aligning money, people and rules with a sharper certainty, and relate this formula of competitive frugality to the needs of the climate crisis.

NEW, QUIETER CAPITALISTS ARE THE SOCIAL RESPONSE CAPITALISTS

The portrayal and the activities of corporate titans seemed to change in the years leading up to 2000, and the eventual financial meltdown of 2007. These birds of prey began to emphasize their reluctance to use their claws. In the next chart, watch how bp thinks of itself in terms of major cities, key corporate partnerships, and in alliance with three giant industrial partners in heavy transport, heavy industry, and high tech.

ALIGNING MONEY, PEOPLE & RULES

Leaders excel today by doing more with teams by habitually aligning money, people and rules daily. These are the three fuels of the leader's bank account, not just dollars and cents.

Leaders feel comfortable in balancing on this tight rope over a snake's pit.

This is what changed the mix of prejudices to allow the growing triumph of the social response capitalists, as I see recent history. Now you can revisit the next chart to see how Looney's focus areas changes our natural forms of consumerism, and makes us think about the needs of business in society, not against society.

A new margin of tolerance defines these first two decades of the twenty-first century. This "margin of new tolerance" allowed and enabled some surprising new twists in the storylines about wealth and the commonwealth. Without claws, these low visibility apologists for rampant capitalism focused mostly on tax and legislation, rather than exploitation and corruption. More and more in society were expecting more and more from business leaders.

By the end of the twentieth century, a widely shared social contract emerged wherein business and society, wealth and the commonwealth, were perceived as intimately related. It was no longer about the ways the rich rigged the system of government for their own benefit (a nineteenth-century preoccupation). Instead, it was about what their excess capital could do for social good.

Looney disclosed the multi-city, multi-year approach to bring bp as a business more in line with the needs of society.

The emergence of broadly appealing not-for-profits added another twist. You can see in the master books of twenty-first century a functional composite emerging from thousands of separate labor and governmental rules. Look to England and the US as pivoting the most here,

bp's FOCUS AREAS

CITIES

10-15 cities prioritized based on:
- **Commitment** to decarbonize
- Existing **relationships** with bp
- Potential to **integrate and reshape** regional energy systems

PARTNERSHIPS

We will collaborate with partners to provide the complementary skills and capabilities that our customers need

CORPORATIONS

3 industrial sectors:
- High tech and consumer products
- Heavy transport
- Heavy industry

Prioritized based on:
- **Scale** of emissions
- **Aligned ambitions** towards net zero
- Potential for **symbiotic and strategic** relationships

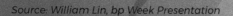

Source: William Lin, bp Week Presentation

bp's JOURNEY

FROM START-UP TO ESTABLISHED BUSINESS

TODAY

Clean Cities and Corporates

- **Launch a new team** to create integrated energy and mobility solutions
- Strategy **focused on 10-15 cities and 3 industrial sectors**
- Working in partnership with Houston, Microsoft and Aberdeen
- Continue to build **momentum and capabilities and new business models** with increasing city and corporate customers aligned with our strategy
- Create **trusted network of partners** that complement our offer

2030

- Be recognized as the **market leader and partner of choice in decarbonization** of cities, corporates and industries

Source: William Lin, bp Week Presentation

in contrast to a steadier understanding in Japan and Australia. For many, opinions shifted about child labor in the States, where the theme that society and business needed to support the poor became accepted and promoted by business in the last six decades of the twentieth century. While a minority of critiques still claimed business the culprit for poverty, increasing numbers of non-profits constructed well-financed boards of directors to promote the opposite view.

Suddenly capitalism was not simply about oil or excess, it was about value creation in a social setting. This is another way to help define the paths to climate competitiveness.

That is what has been missed too often since the last financial meltdown: The people who are profiting also believe in investing along the lines of environmental, social and governance metrics. As noted in our introduction, this ESG movement is now domineering the oil valuations. While it is still a term of some debate, ESG is something you can see of social value in how bp positions itself for change. I find this hard to write about because every day the issues are hotly debated in the press and in the boardrooms I serve; yet what is clear is that the winners are those on the path of climate competitiveness, and the losers are those refusing the new ESG monies. (For more, see my book *New World Companies* on the future of capitalism, where we examine the primary financial institutions and investment house enabling this broad and important claim.)

VIVID VERSUS RAW THEMES

One of the key partners Looney describes is Microsoft, as a great giant enabler of further decarbonization through better data and smarts.

There are significant changes resulting in climate action in legislation these days, from the CHIPS bill, to the infrastructure bill. These changes are evident in market and in social dynamics. For example, before the passage of the historic Inflation Reduction Act, over 11 percent of the United States land mass was preserved for parks, land easements, or conservancies. Yet the Biden administration began a low visibility campaign to address climate change by preserving 30 percent of our land mass. This enables more carbon capture, less pollution of gas magnifiers, as well as fulfills the human need for outside recreation and more biodiversity.

WEALTH SURROUNDS

This propels me to my next point: real wealth surrounds. It compounds a life that is well spent. This wealth is an existential fact of the curious life; and if you let it, it makes you feel creative, too.

Freud called this the call of civilization, the superego at play. Darwin saw it in the natural struggle for survival.

There are books about the rampant spread of newspapers, reading in libraries, and public concerts in the time after Marx, Freud, and Darwin. What was once mostly an elite domain of the wealthy, today musical preferences are universal.

SCALING-UP NEXT-GEN MOBILITY BUSINESS

Success Factors

- **Fast and convenient** charging
- **Most efficient** price setter
- **Digital solutions** and **loyalty**
- **Strategic partnerships**
- **Advantaged** network

LEADING **NEXT-GEN MOBILITY** BUSINESS

Customers at home

Rapid and ultra-fast charging

Public charging

Destination charging

H₂ Hydrogen mobility solutions

Fleet mobility solutions

>70,000
EV charge points by 2030

Convenience and Mobility, bp week, Sept. 2020

What Looney is leading at bp and his peer competitors changes world view; it also changes our sense of mobility and what empowers this new age of carbon constraints. We go from a five-minute gas station filling to a view of the convenience store as having enough for your family to allow fifteen-minute recharging with an electric infrastructure of cars and trucks. It allows the building from 7,000 gas stations to 70,000 global touch points. This increase in the many ways bp touches other people and businesses underlines the social significance of these changes from big oil into a cleaner energy company. In what you see next, you can reimagine, as Looney does, the aims of your travel plans, along the lines of a more climate responsive transportation infrastructure. If you look closely, you can see this happening in America, Canada, throughout London and England, in Singapore, in Africa, and now in Australia. It would be wrong-headed to assume this is nothing short of magnificent and a monumental change, for after 120 years of big oil, the change is now before us. The elephant is marching in a new more climate-responsive direction.

This relentless pursuit of imaginative and creative improvement is what Sigmund Freud called "the call of civilization." Yet modern neuroscientists suggest this is a native part of everyone in youth, that sometimes gets factored out in professionalism.

That call tightens the belt around the young violin player in Korea or Vietnam until she is concert ready. That call makes the young writer refuse rejection and persist. This call of civilization is what Freud in his books in the 1920s, at the end of his productive life, explained as "sublimation."

My point is you can feel wealthy even when poor. Bernard Looney came to power after bp dropped from a near 300 billion market cap to below 89 billion due to the Gulf Spill in America. It was in the social context of this known humbling of the old bp where a leader like a Looney could emerge, and triumph in his big energy and social leadership skills.

He had to embody the principles of doing more with less not only to survive but also to thrive in this new era calling for climate competitiveness.

YET, WE DO NEED ENOUGH EXCESS

Modern men and women need enough excess. Let me repeat that. We not only need accuracy and science, and law, we also need the excesses of civilization.

This does not mean you go to a concert or play on Broadway every night of the week. Instead, it means you can read and listen as you wish, each day, for very little. Wealth surrounds us. We do not thrive in spare lives—we need enough excess. While I preach competitive frugality in my firm and family, I never meant a withdrawal from the wealth of the arts and civilization.

Freud taught me that there are several imperatives in human longing and ambition. One is brute force, the id, the animal instinct, that which remains in the brain chemistry even after 5,000 years of civilization. Another force is the ego, which Freud accurately portrayed as a "mediating force." Today the wellness movement and the good will of many try to downplay the sheer intensity of ego in each of us, yet the ego is a mediating force even when someone tries to repress it. And then of course there is the superego, what Freud names as the call of civilization. I believe it is in everyone, thus the instinct for craftsmanship.

The need for money-making is one thing, but the instinct for doing a craft well is deeper than that first need. Freud is right, even today. His claims that there is something in human nature—in the everyday life of being human—where we fill up with longing, unfulfilled wishes, and darker drives is still relevant.

Freud's classic *Civilization and Its Discontents* explains two other fundamental points to this book's domain. He explains why repression works; and he explains why repression can be outsmarted by creative pressures and strong will.

Think of the athlete at the edge of fatigue who wins; think of the musician on a world tour, performing despite exhaustion; think of the book writer offering something that sells for less than a dinner. Why do folks do this? Well, it is the call for civilization. Civilization is based on just competition.

We need to sum up some key points here.

1. Wealth surrounds. That explains why the creative class can discover a lasting demonstration on wealth and the commonwealth in the many centuries of the human experience.

TRANSFORMATION AND STRATEGIC INTENT

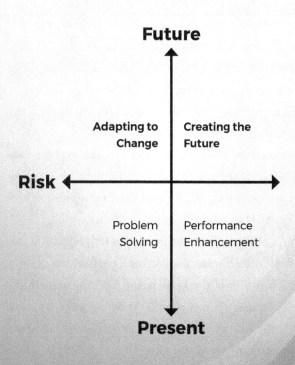

Future

Adapting to Change

Creating the Future

Risk

Problem Solving

Performance Enhancement

Present

Source: Gord Lambert, AHC Group

2. Humans, especially modern twenty-first-century humans, conflate the historic set of complex virtues into a set of simpler conflated prejudices about competition and about rights of the individual. Many in the acts of pre-judgment take the higher facts of the interplay of society and business and conflate them into self-defeating decisions of waste and excess, leading to further addictions to the petrochemical treadmill we are trying to step off. If you avoid this simple conflation into prejudice, consciously, and build a new narrative of climate solutions, instead of climate dread or denial, you begin to profit and to answer social needs at the same time.

3. This leads us to understand the value in social movements that fight against the wealthy to assert the universal rights of environmental, social, and governance needs.

For this transition, it is good enough to hold in your mind why I believe "we need enough excess." Without enough excess, our rules and our policies are presented as draconian. We need wiggle room to apply the principles of competitive frugality. Why? Because it is hard to meet the needs of complex climate change solutions, and the needs of the commonwealth, without some room for error and inventive experimentation.

> *We all live in a swift and severe world, where speed of information sparks off more questions than answers hourly. Leaders habitually embrace being ad-*

ept in the short run, and adaptive in the long, so all their energy and time is expended on seeking shareable solutions.

Pay attention to these three magical principles in your life of doing more with less. It is the purpose of this book to have you realign, as Looney did, the purposes of money, people, and rules in your life.

A FEW TALES THAT DEFEAT THE POPULAR PREJUDICES

"I feel the joy of your first daughter in you," my doctoral candidate Stephen Kendie said to me, early one morning, as we walked the campus of Rensselaer Institute of Technology. Stephen, a prince from Ghana, was in the third year of a funded study of implementation gaps in financing water systems to fight water-borne diseases in Ghana and Togo. He was an ideal graduate student, among many, and an ideal family man, too.

Unlike the hurried immature graduate students that abounded from America and other lands in my graduate program, there was a humble quietude in Stephen. He would stop, grinning, and ask me on any day: "How is your family? How is your wife? How is your body?" He had a special expansive exploring mind that roamed into a heavy reading of piles of books and reports I gave him each week.

Stephen had a deep respect for daily wonders, for those doing so much with so little in his region of the world. He was not distracted by his wealth or his readiness as a prince—he did not even have a car during his years at RPI. Instead, I noticed him living steps away from campus, near where I parked my car, thus providing us many encounters in the morning outside of the classes we shared. Often, the exchange was the most miraculous part of my day.

I thought of Stephen this year while preparing to complete the last few passages in this book. Part of doing more with less is to read into other cultures, to grow more creative and more inclusive in our actions and results.

Part of doing more with less is making prayer of the best conversations, learning about our better selves in them. The point of this book is that wealth surrounds you—no matter your economic or educational status—everyday, when we get back to basic humanity. This satisfies our needs of the everyday. For Stephen, doing more with less was success.

LARGER LESSONS FROM LESS

You cannot generalize from one great doctoral candidate, nor can you generalize from one representative tale about many miracles like that in our corporate cases of bp or Trane. Life demands—as does your sense of social history—more complex reactions than ones based on a few cases.

Yet you can productively speculate on their relevance for a future where droughts abound, oceans rise, and temperatures hurt more and more. That is the social imperative that is changing the ratio of wealth to the commonwealth, and the responsibilities of business to society. Businesses that will succeed will need to do more than simply answer the needs of their customers, and the return expectations of their immediate stockholders.

I have been investing in over 175 stocks over the last twenty years, and I have worked with three wealth management advisory firms. From this experience, I began to visualize a better balance between wealth and the commonwealth. I find many of my best performing stocks teach, in hints and indirection, about what I now call these arts of competitive frugality.

Here is my take-away from traveling the world with my eyes wide open: It does not matter if your staff resides in Mecca, Africa, Long Island, Silicon Valley, or Dublin. You need to discover the wealth in you. Think of that focus phrase deeply: the need to discover the wealth in you.

When you think back across the first passages of this book, you may recall how often we used classic books like Thoreau or Freud to capture a probable lived experience in you, the reader. We did this to assert a few basic principles on the path to competitive frugality and climate competitiveness.

We suggested that the phrase "climate competitiveness" has many different company-based definitions. For bp, it means a fundamental shift in energy sales and selection. In Trane, it means bringing the outside megatrends inside, through human resources retraining.

The lesson of recent social history is that all firms must rachet down their contributions to greenhouse gas emissions. And that part of your worth remains in finding your role in this path.

The new narrative on business and society requires your voice and your vigilant set of choices.

I've come to think our new narrative suggests that wealth is available to those willing to work for it, and not waste it. This is the great moral of our modern times. There is an abundance of natural and civic wealth before you. Inspire the next generation.

CARE OF THE YOUNG AS A SIGN OF COMPOUNDING VALUE

Care of the young is a critical element to this book. We cannot close such a book without making more of how a changed youth represents compounding values to society and the future of business.

Sharing wealth with the next generation is fundamental in all cultures, from the ancient ones in Africa and Arabia to ones of newly minted nations or firms. Here we simply offer you the essential competitive principles, where care of the young becomes the icon of what is needed.

When we watch children learn we can often see the wonder in their eyes, and the concentration when the tales being told to them let their imaginations fly.

Active undulating flight—the vistas of ascension to the clouds and the unbounded freedoms it suggests—is probably the single most vivid quality that connects birds to the human spirit. While the prejudices of adults narrow and blind, the aspirations of the young are about learning at times, or trying, simply because they can. Prejudice over time gives adults an active resistance to happiness. The adult feels not wealthy enough, or smart enough, or adequate enough to satisfy their expectations of family or firm. But a child, as seen below, can be lost in fascination. Regain in your life, no matter your age or family needs, this youthful curiosity in frugality and the doing of good, and your life will begin again in this age of climate change.

Some basics on children:

1. Besides the beautiful fact that most young children do not care a bit about differences between the wealthy leisure society and normal society, there is a huge ugly impact on the fate of youth due to these prejudices.

2. Kids are not born with socioeconomic prejudices, or destinies. Yet their fate, and their freedoms, are curtailed by prejudiced adults. I believe to conquer the numbing complexities of climate science and industrial reinvention, we need to restore the child's wonder in the pursuit. Let children teach adults more here.

However, if you begin to teach the children the power of competitive frugality within their family, community and in the larger arenas of society, you enable proper growth and a return to basic civics. This enables young adults to discover the value of savings and compounded interest, for example, something critical in this age of so much debt and waste and wrongdoing. It is one of the most humble and assured ways to become independent and wealthy by the first phases of old age; yet denying this financial literacy to most children is like robbing their piggy banks through their teens.

It is not a hard concept. We had our daughter Colette have three piggy banks—one for herself, one for her immediate friends, and one for the near future of those in need. That seemed to get through, from the wonder years of age eight to her entry to medical school, a very expensive venture she entered with intelligent frugality.

My mother, a factory worker, taught me the same values, where we never felt poor despite being below the poverty line most of my first twenty years. As recorded in my memoir *Missing Persons*, my mother's stories were rich, as were her friendships. My wife's family, working-class folks who believed in higher education, sent five kids to college with the wages of a trucker. That takes the arts of competitive frugality and compounding interest.

That is why doing more with less creates a set of reinforcing concentric circles, starting with the frugal self, going out to family, then friends, and then your firm, and eventually the firms you impact that are much larger than your firm.

SEEKING A BALANCE BETWEEN PAST MISTAKES AND PRESENT PREDICAMENTS

The path of climate competitiveness is strengthened again when we involve youth, yet is weakened when we slip back into the past prejudices and mistakes of speculative capitalism, a perennial problem—as evident this year of 2023 by the failures in the Silicon Valley Bank. This is why the principles of this book are a better bet than speculative capitalism, and a more secure way to wealth.

The problem E. F. Schumacher taught me is that we need "economics with a human face," not just balance sheets and margins of profit. When speculative capitalists tell their wage earners that they are nothing but a wage earner, you put them in a box of self-defeat. That is why the path of speculative capitalists is always slippery.

If we teach children properly, in the spirit of these folk tales like Robin Hood, children of this climate change age are our grounds for hope in a near future.

Children will embody the competitive principles of knowing how to do so much with so little. That is why society is not just high society, as advertisers and rampant speculative capitalists in magazines like *Vanity Fair* would have you assume.

Once the new generation thinks like Stephen Kendi, they will realize that wealth surrounds us all, and for some, the miracles are many. It is then that we can begin to solve more climate challenges and offer a sensible competitive new narrative on sustainability solutions.

Many folk tales share common, universally human pragmatic themes. Some suggest that every citizen can gain wealth in one's lifetime through the community, through civic involvement. When Albert Einstein stated in his mature years: "Strive not to be a success, but to be of value," he was expressing a fundamentally sound idea that the children of the world can and should adopt the age of climate impacts in order to survive. Many of the other tales are about the principles of being self-actualizing, not the abstract virtues of being enlightened.

And why does this matter to our age of climate change of global pressures? Because it improves society as it improves the self. That is the key to the shared genius in the principles stated in these passages. Think of this century where we need to balance on the surfboard of business and society. Current and the new generation require a basic class in civics and pragmatic values. I know this is not my place to make such a sweeping claim, but I do so with a touch of humility. The world would be less severe and less swift if we re-achieved this balance in our civilization. You can return to the basics of civics by teaching the young that the age of oil is essentially over. There is a need to use oil transitionally, but the age of superabundance of oil and gas is over, even when we factor in the promise of hydrogen and liquified natural gas.

I have found that corporate life is full of tricksters. Being shortsighted involves tricking yourself on the dictates of social history. And we think this prepares us for a swift and mounting world of climate concerns, like waves hitting the shores.

Humanity wants a balance between wealth and the commonwealth, and a return to the basics of civics. The waves of change are redefining the direction of both business purpose and social need.

It would be wrong to misread these signals of change. A large elephant of change is marching forward, changing tax policy on oil, changing technology to cleaner forms of energy, changing markets and the patterns of investment. As you now sense, this complex of changes in technology, markets, investments, and policy require a creative force found in both youthful curiosity and the march of social history as rendered here.

WHAT ROBIN HOOD TELLS US ABOUT CLIMATE COMPETITIVENESS

It is not what you say, it is what they hear! This insight is one of the key discoveries of the last century. From marketing strategies to neuroscience research, more and more we have come to validate that what we communicate is not just received on its basic facts. It is absorbed through the human psyche and experience, so that the impact of our message is just as much felt as understood, more so in fact.

And one of the most effective ways we communicate with each other, and move our society forward, is through stories and fables that endure.

I believe we're approaching a new era in which significant progress on climate change (and other social issues) can be made. Since the 2007 financial crisis, the

disruptive promise of the environmental, social, and governance movement has taken hold in the business world.
The passing of the Inflation Reduction Act, which includes over $400 billion in climate solution technologies
and subsidies, is another big step forward.

These two recent Titan-like giant steps help many off
the petrochemical treadmill. I hear the rumbles of that
"stepping off the treadmill" each day in my practice with
firms. Yet the social meaning of these developments can
now be felt and understood more widely. The big-step
changes have begun to happen in investment markets,
in national policies, and in global corporations. But they
are not yet fully appropriated by story into the popular
culture. Therefore, some disabling prejudices against carbon competitiveness remain in the popular imagination,
damaging remnants from the past, despite the progress
on integrating business with society.

After reviewing the historic trends, I believe many—
the majority of humans across 192 nations—are now
ready for serious action on climate change. We see this
in the surveys by Globe Scan internally, and by George
Mason University's work with Yale and Stanford survey
teams. Attitude and urgency indicators have changed,
but confusion on action paths remain. This takes us beyond the simple 360.org and divestment campaigns of
recent decades into a whole new world of solutions and
innovation. People want a new narrative of solutions.

If intelligently applied, these forces can form the
spinal storyline of a new narrative on climate solutions.

What is at stake is a needed, smart, and fair rebalance of wealth between the wealthy and the vast majority in the commonwealth.

But it can't simply be preached. It will require a new narrative, a shared story we work from together, of what it takes to succeed by doing more with less.

As the last 120 years of big oil have demonstrated again and again, you cannot defeat greenhouse magnifiers and the complexities of manmade climate impacts through law, technology, and markets alone. You need to influence the pace of consumption and the feelings shared across the collective. That is what we have been calling "The Social Needs of the Commonwealth" in this and all my books since 1990. People of expertise often ask me what I mean by social needs, yet I find most people know exactly what that means. Only the elites and experts seem uncertain.

But how do we form this new narrative, a tale of how we can right the imbalances that hold us back? Luckily, we have an example, right in front of us. For what story resonates these ideas better than the tale of Robin Hood?

FIRST, A WARNING

Before we delve into Robin Hood, we can speak some about the very essence of story and myth. Folk tales can be poisonous, even when people first see them as entertainment. This is because the narrative elements resonate emotionally for those hidden and repressed, liberating a sense of energy and concern and passion for action.

A deep fable is different from a deep dig or excavation in the physical world. A fable's depth resides in the collective psyche and in your mindful emotions. Some technical and engineering types, I have found, doubt if there is such a thing as a collective psyche. If this is you, please think then of this as a historical popular myth. This status as a framing of higher shared cultural facts is key for "the stories we need" to outmaneuver the brutal force built into the petrochemical treadmill.

A good effective tale makes you think globally, about your family, your friends, your firm. It is rapidly shared across different age groups and social levels.

Through the ages we remember Robin Hood—and other tales of social advocates—for solid social reasons. When we experience, as readers, tales like those of Robin Hood, something happens throughout our brain. The response is not simply rational. We embrace the entertainment punch of the fable with open heart and a more open mind, freeing ourselves of pre-judgment. The response, the neuroscientists show us, is more like when we enjoy music. Tales and music stimulate action in many parts of our brain, not just the language functions. These tales, from any culture, get us past our simple prejudices into a realm of the collective socialized self—the commonwealth.

By examining a tale like Robin Hood through the ages, we suggest that a higher truth needs to be embraced the rest of this century: It is that frugality requires a kind of militancy. The arts of competitive frugality—the entirety of the ESG movements—constitute, through billions of investment clicks, a kind of "stealing from the rich to give to the poor." These investment militants are being like Robin Hood in more nefarious ways, as they are embarrassing the wasteful and the leisurely to take climate change seriously through tens of thousands of clicks per a trading day, globally.

This began after the 2007 financial crisis. You can see its impact on capital markets and corporates. Yet the popular imagination still lags behind.

ROBIN HOOD THROUGH THE YEARS

J. C. Holt wrote the most comprehensive account of the legend of Robin Hood. It pays to itemize some of the historic lessons for our age.

1. Robin Hood as a surname in England appeared as early as 1296. To me that means the tale has saliency for at least 700 years, if not before. This was the time Dante was writing about business and society in Italia. Both Dante's *Divine Comedy* and the stories about Robin Hood are classics in exploring business and society, wealth within the commonwealth, when you read them properly, as lasting cultural fables.

2. Holt explains how this tale about wealth justice and injustice led to the creation of Robin Hood mimics in the popular May festivals. There is plenty of historic evidence about church festivities celebrating Robin Hood. By the sixteenth century, the figure of

Robin was very British, even on Flag Day! Yet what matters is how great folk tales spring up new roots in many different nations and regions.

3. Holt wants us to understand that his book is about a legend rather than a man. I want you to understand that the proper fulcrum to balance wealth and the commonwealth resides in your worldview and actions, not in government policy or corporate behavior. We need policy and improved technology, but more so we need to embrace the mind-shift that only fable enables.

4. Holt asserts: "The identity of the man matters less than the persistence of the legend. That is the most remarkable thing about him." This makes me think of the legend of Gandhi, how his legend grew after his assassination. It also makes me think about how the tale of George Floyd is morphing into something larger than life.

5. Holt explains how the legend "snowballed, collecting fragments of other stories as it rolled along." Even "the central character was re-modelled. At his first appearance Robin was a yeoman. He was then turned into a nobleman unjustly deprived of his inheritance, later into an Englishman protecting his native countryman from the domination of the Normans."

These ideas of economic revenge evolved as the image of Robin Hood changed, even up to the 1960s when he became like a quintessential social rebel. His hair grew long, flowing in the winds.

6. Holt goes on, saying: "At first sight the legend is about justice. Robin is at once an embodiment of honor and an agent of retribution. He corrects the evil which flows from the greed of rich clerics and the corruption of the royal officials." But here is the key point for this book: "But he does not seek to overturn social conventions. On the contrary, Robin Hood sustains these conventions against the machinations of the wicked and the powerful who explicitly flout and undermine them."

Points one through six constitute, in my experience, the elements of the new narrative we all now need to sing along with. I cannot place enough emphasis on the subtle appropriation significance in point six, that the tale "does not seek to overturn social conventions." That is its genius in melding solution paths between the dominant culture and its emerging and reactionary cultures.

Throughout the centuries that the tale of Robin Hood has been told, and all its evolutions over time, a few key characteristics always remain the same:

1. Robin Hood keeps his word before his brethren, while the treacherous sheriff does not. He is portrayed as an emerging new man, while the clerics, the nobles, and the sheriff are fixed.

2. Robin Hood is always presented as doing more with less, as frugal, alert, and clever. In fact, all dramas of Robin Hood become brilliant when we begin to see him as light on his feet! In episode after episode, he

is presented as nimbler than the indulgent clerics and administrators making a villain of him. I take this to mean that Robin Hood is not burdened with heavy baggage. Instead, he is light and capable of doing much more with less.

That is why at the end of the Holt's book he asserts: "Robin stands outside the law as an honorable criminal, and the audience is asked to take the outlaw's side." Think here of Nelson Mandela, his cause being made universal by the Truth and Reconciliation councils led by Desmond Tutu.

3. Most important, Robin Hood is a generous human being. He wins our hearts and minds by taking what is criminal and giving it back to the poor in a magical transformation of generosity. We do not think of him as a criminal, as we no longer think of Nelson Mandela as "criminal" or Henry David Thoreau as subversive.

It is my belief that all who want to see progress in the coming years, especially climate change advocates, must find a way to become a new Robin Hood in our culture. They must be seen just as trustworthy, frugal, and generous as our cultural hero. They must return us to our basic civics, (not only what critics call a deep ecology).

This return to a basic humanity in our midst does not cost us much. It involves liberating a narrative where civics is based on balancing wealth and the commons in a way that delights, not divides. Climate competitiveness engages these more positive forces in social change. Again, this happens in the new narrative without revolution or social chaos. In fact, the opposite happens. Societies across the nations re-achieve the lost balance between business and society, between wealth and the common-wealth, in ways that redistribute wealth to those that are climate competitive, and others lose. This is the new way of the world, although you can hear the complaints daily.

THE STAGES OF A SOCIAL MOVEMENT

We are at a pivotal point in our history of struggles with addressing climate change. The Inflation Reduction Act embodies that shift of attitude, a shift to a deeper pur-pose of actions in our homes, our cars, and our energy infrastructure.

In our age of carbon and capital constraints, the world is now ready to adopt this shift. We've entered a new age of the human role in nature, one of caritas. We have left the prejudices of the past about petroleum. We are about to explore an entirely new world of clean energy and lifestyle changes. While my emphasis here is on the American new legislation, parallel changes have occurred in Europe, Asia, and the Island economies of this world.

We need now think a bit more about the historic processes that drive social movements. Think here about how it took years for FDR to enter the fight against the fire of Hitler in Europe and the world. Think here how it takes years, even decades, for most social movements to simmer before the boil. The moment we are reaching on climate change also has decades of slower movement behind it. This is how social movements advance.

BACK TO BASICS

The art of living a frugal life and running a frugal firm is the best way to be a Robin Hood in this time of climate change. In short, you must learn to thrive profitably and reliably through doing more with less.

In re-achieving balance between wealth and the needs of the commonwealth for this new century, we need to make complex tradeoffs to thrive in a time of climate change. As I indicated to experts and corporates in earlier books, it will take a Ben Franklin-like pragmatism to get there, a set of trade-offs aligning money, people, and rules.

The cunning and cleverness of a Robin Hood mindset can be your own protest song. Robin Hood's tale suggests that the clever can be made heroic before the masses. For example, Nelson Mandela is a Robin Hood. He was a prisoner, but a prisoner of an unjust system. He was always seen by those who wrote about him as patient, clever, and warm. He outsmarted the prejudices of the dominant culture.

Similarly, Robin Hood shows how one can enact change through similar cunning and flair:

It is the combination of his risk and daring, mixed with his social returns, that allow the fabulous elements in the fable of Robin Hood.

It is Robin Hood's love of justice mixed with adventure that compels, not just his advocacy of justice.

He would rather outsmart the dominant culture than revolutionize it. Unlike the preachers of the apocalypse, this new protest song, this work of the troubadour, turns those with a narrative of newly refined rules on their head. In business terms, this takes a realignment of money people and rules. In public discourse, it involves a celebrated and appropriated mind shift.

We begin to listen and to respond, as my mentor Gordon Lambert of Canada notes, rather than simply "study and declare."

Because no moment in history is ever completely free of a dominant culture, an emergent culture, and a reactionary culture. It is not in the cards. The tales that stand tall over time are those with a more complex drama to them than simply "good defeats evil." Robin Hood, with his merry pranksters, is such a tale.

These tales survive because of human failings. Things like gullibility and self-deception abound as subthemes in all folk tales. While we need science and policy to compel us into a more frugal world, at the same time we need to be ready to outsmart the self-deceptions of the smug and the rich, and that requires cunning not just logic.

This informs why the environmental movement must broaden past its initial 1970s form of leisure-class smugness, into a more universal and inclusive set of social imperatives.

Nowadays, there is a deep impatience built into the public regarding climate change responses. You can see this vividly in a note Dr. Edward Maibach provided to me in July 2022. "The data from our new survey showing that 58% of American voters (including 48% of moderate Republicans) want the President to declare a climate emergency IF CONGRESS DOES NOT ACT." Visit the webpages of the Medical Consortium on Public Health and Climate for a rich sample of science, policy, and insight.

Professor Edward Maibach was profoundly right in his claim. By August 8 of that same summer of 2022, Congress acted to pass the Inflation Reduction Act, passing over $560 billion in climate solution technologies and subsidies. (See our company webpage, **www.ahcgroup. com**, for details on these matters.) When you examine the evidence, this will get massive money and massive changes underway by the years 2030 and 2040. We as a world will be close to climate competitiveness in our transportation infrastructure, in our building science, in our manufacturing systems, and in our supply chain.

This book's time horizon coincides by design with the implementation of these large acts on infrastructure and the Inflation Reduction Act, both passed by bi-partisan force in Congress, and widely supported by the press and the general public, although there are, of course, a few divergent views.

GOOD TROUBLE

The balance of what is good for the commonwealth and what is bad behavior of the wealthy changes over time. Overall, the intolerance of idle waste increases through this century. In the end, the tale of Robin Hood is a tale of defiance. But it is also a beginning with each new person "getting the tale's impact."

It is my hope that this book will put you in the same shared frame of mind. The age of climate and capital constraints requires no less. "Doing more with less" is the mantra of this century's success stories.

THE NEW NARRATIVE

In this book I have striven to provide a bird's-eye view of the last 120 years of industrial history. During this fly over, I attempted to explain why it is so easy to fall into any of the five prejudices described at the start of this book. Yet the point was to dramatize the exemplar behavior on the path to solutions.

Popular delusions on wealth are not the same as a psychological personal delusion. They are more evasive, as they are widely shared. But this book is not about those popular delusions. Instead, the book is about actions and attitudes that are more insidious. These popular prejudices have deceived and distorted lives for too long. It is time to return to a set of human-scale ambitions dictated by corporate industriousness, social care, and personal and competitive frugality.

At the beginning of this book, I asked you to think about the popular narratives on business and society, which expose the innards of how these two must live together to solve our problems. I promised that we'd take a nose-dive at those prejudices to heal our wounds. While not wanting to be mean or blameful, I tried to expose the innards of these prejudices as we flew over the large contours of our recent industrialized past.

As we conclude, there are some fundamentals that I hope to share with you now, to summarize my beliefs:

1. Large segments of society have discovered how the prejudices of wealth can be erased and restated.

2. We now have a historic opportunity to step beyond the petrochemical treadmill into a cleaner, more just (socially inclusive), and more vivid future for many.

Over each chapter, we dissected some of the more visible nerves entangled within the muscles of these prejudices, both from those looking up to the wealthy, and from the point of view of the wealthy looking down at the populace. That constituted the analytical parts of the book.

But we also looked to more sweeping and tale-based insights—looking from Africa to Robin Hood—that can inform you into the new personal narratives now required.

These noted developments take us to a tipping point, beyond the current edge in history.

I feel all the weight of the past mistakes are redeemable with a basic return to the humanism that abounds around us in nature, in arts, culture and music, and in our protest songs.

Here is a step process moving forward:

1. We can restore the original humane sense of civics to a majority of consumers, in all nations, and in swift order. Consumers, in doing more with less, must become citizens again.

2. This act of social value and civics forms a kind of historic pivot point in the new narrative. You can feel the edge of this pivot point. Celebrate in your music and your day this fulcrum of change.

3. What was once a series of separate social movements, now in balance, can achieve a functional unity of purpose, as climate solutions make a world in action on the net zero journey. Today massive AI and diagnostic systems allow this alignment for the shared new narrative.

4. "E Pluribus Unum" is now the chant of modern industrialized society, not just of our democracies.

Many billions of citizens, not just the super-rich or consumptive leisurely class, know how to return to this premise of the social contract: from many comes one voice. This new narrative can realign the sovereign energy-producing nations with the more frugal seeking change under communistic and socialist regimes. I can see this emerging in the honorable strength of the Ukraine fighters against Putin, as competitive frugality and open governments are the new requirement to compete in world markets.

5. With the snap of a few good global fables (like that of Robin Hood), we can revitalize a full generation in their imagination.

   This has happened at pivot points in history, where the collective force of the dominant, emergent, and reactionary cultures crash into the key rocks, pushing them upstream.

6. There remains a miracle we can observe in social histories, as shifts of consequence create the betterment of most people over time. Life has gotten longer for most; our rights have been extended, and our role in technological wonders has continued to rise. Sure, there are problems, but this is a book of answers.

7. With the wave of a hand, the magic of innovation and clean energy can happen, once the cobwebs of the fossil fuel petrochemical treadmill are turned completely off in our entrenched prejudices.

We can get back to basics. The principles of social history can provide us the strength of character to align these changes. We base these bold claims on social history not personal preferences.

Ulysses S. Grant noted at the end of his great *Personal Memoir*, "I feel that we are at the eve of a new era."

In a similar fashion, I feel we are at the eve of a new era in the relationships between business and society.

This new era, despite all the division in our politics and world views, will enable progress on the path of climate competitiveness.

It is as if the elephant of social history will march forward with advances in cleaner technologies, in better performing investment and capital markets that support climate responsiveness, and in the ways policy and mandates happen in a new supportive rather than simply regulatory fashion. I've called for these changes in all my books, but now they are happening in the world of social change. That is why I, like Grant, believe that a new era has begun.

Rereading Samet's *Annotated Memoirs of Ulysses S. Grant*, I conclude a higher lesson as a student of social history. Humans are lost until our general public accepts and learns how to ask the tough questions of war, its astute preparations that the great generals like Grant understood, its profound realignments of money, soldiers, and their military rules, allowing the complex of purposes after diplomacy fails. No one feels comfort in war. Similarly, no one feels complete comfort in how business and society must interact to solve our climate crisis, and will.

After completing this twenty-second book of mine on business and society, I have concluded something in reflecting on my memoir and my career in business in this supporting summary book:

Humans will remain lost regarding climate challenges until we learn to ask "the tough questions" about wealth and its relationship to climate competitiveness. At the beginning of this book I've isolated the five prejudices that have distorted our ability to ask these questions, until of late.

THE ELEPHANT IN THE ROOM

What this new narrative requires, to be visual and sportive, is the wisdom and persistence of what I call "the elephant in the room."

I visualize this large social change before us, like the face of this elephant. It is wise, stubborn, and with new forward momentum. This elephant, like social history itself moving us into a path of climate competitiveness, requires a set of stern and clever step changes, a moving forward with strong momentum we now see in our capital markets and new cleaner technologies. It is a stern but clever step change, four giant limbs of policy, technology, markets, and investments all in better moving forward.

In my own hometown of Saratoga, the strongest naval empire of the British empire was stopped in the Battle of Saratoga to end the Revolutionary period. Ukraine resistance, now a European and American joint effort, is showing another revolution against the autocrat Putin. These historic pivot points are now occurring more quietly, but as reliably, in the themes outlined above.

SUMMING UP THE GIANT STEPS FORWARD

In my own life, the rights of many disenfranchised groups have been vividly elevated. You can feel a new form of openness in the new generation of my daughter and her friends.

I am not saying our society has been completely integrated—we see this each day in our neighborhoods and our news feed—disenfranchised groups still have a long road ahead. But you would be a blind reactionary if you cannot see and feel these changes coming, with force and result. I believe in my heart and soul that the elite—which trained me from Cornell to the corporate mansions I worked within—cannot resist such force in social movements any longer. We can rebalance wealth and the commonwealth without violent revolutions.

I am not the only social historian or book writer who sees these changes in vivid color. As a student of social history and social movements since college, I do not buy all the current media and copy on our extremes. Turn off that static radio and involve yourself in the beauty that abounds in nature, in the arts, culture, and music.

Of course, there are counter views. That is what makes open governments continue to improve. Extremes sell weaker newspapers and win well-viewed TV appearances, but these arguments do not really move the vast spectrum of people. All this screaming into the internet has little real-world impact. Our new narrative will get us back to the basis of civics, E PLURIBUS UNUM.

From many factions, there will be one purpose and voice. Expect debates. Expect divisions and factions. But also expect unifying actions in communities on climate change and other social movements.

While I cannot break confidentiality agreements, please note I do alert my global clients like Warren Buffet's Shaw Industries, and Toyota and Walgreens Boots Alliance that these changes are mounting and that they matter to their competitive advantage. For every graphic you've seen from our stack of supporting documents to clients, please note that each presented has over three dozen supporting facts and market details behind them, that I cannot and will not share from my business practice.

Yet I've left as clear a trail of evidence in the books. Soon you will not be able to operate in a business of any size without this sense of the commonwealth in your actions. See more evidence at **www.worldincbook.com** and **www.ahcgroup.com**.

The biggest confirming point is that these shifts are now evident in public opinion. Note this snapshot on who is trusted in society today (see next page).

Look at how a science-based exploration agency, NASA, is trusted across the board from Liberal Democrats to Conservative Republicans, and that family and friends are also universally held in common esteem, with the

WHO REGISTERED VOTERS TRUST MOST AS SOURCES

RANK BY TRUST	ALL REGISTERED VOTERS	LIBERAL DEMOCRATS
1	NASA	Climate Scientists
2	Family & Friends	Environmental Organizations
3	Climate Scientists	EPA
4	Your Primary Care Doctor	NASA
5	EPA	Teachers
6	Television Weather Reporters	President Biden
7	Environmental Organizations	National Public Radio (NPR)
8	Teachers	Television Weather Reporters
9	American Medical Association	Family & Friends
10	Your Local Newspaper	National Network News
11	National Public Radio (NPR)	American Medical Association
12	Local TV News	Your Local Newspaper
13	Nation Network News	CNN
14	President Biden	Your Primary Care Doctor
15	U.S. Military Leaders	MSNBC
16	CNN	Local TV News
17	MSNBC	Your Congressperson
18	Your Congressperson	U.S. Military Leaders
19	Leaders In Your Religious Faith	Leaders In Your Religious Faith
20	The Fox News Channel	The Fox News Channel
21	Oil, Gas, And Coal Companies	Oil, Gas, And Coal Companies

OF INFORMATION ABOUT GLOBAL WARMING

MODERATE/CONSER-VATIVE DEMOCRATS	LIBERAL/MODERATE REPUBLICANS	CONSERVATIVE REPUBLICANS
Climate Scientists	NASA	Family & Friends
EPA	Family & Friends	Your Primary Care Doctor
Environmental Organizations	Your Primary Care Doctor	NASA
NASA	Climate Scientists	The Fox News Channel
Television Weather Reporters	EPA	Leaders In Your Religious Faith
American Medical Association	Television Weather Reporters	Television Weather Reporters
President Biden	U.S. Military Leaders	Climate Scientists
Your Primary Care Doctor	Teachers	U.S. Military Leaders
National Network News	American Medical Association	American Medical Association
National Public Radio (NPR)	Environmental Organizations	Teachers
Your Local Newspaper	Your Local Newspaper	Oil, Gas, And Coal Companies
Family & Friends	Local TV News	EPA
Local TV News	National Public Radio (NPR)	Your Local Newspaper
Teachers	National Network News	Environmental Organizations
CNN	The Fox News Channel	Your Congressperson
MSNBC	Leaders In Your Religious Faith	Local TV News
U.S. Military Leaders	Your Congressperson	National Public Radio (NPR)
Your Congressperson	CNN	National Network News
Leaders In Your Religious Faith	MSNBC	CNN
Oil, Gas, And Coal Companies	Oil, Gas, And Coal Companies	MSNBC
The Fox News Channel	President Biden	President Biden

ranking of news stations and oil and gas companies near bottom. The elephant walks this path of joint change, not individual difference or preference. The march of social history is larger by far than any of us, and it is this march that will help get more and more companies and people on the path of climate competitiveness in the decades ahead of us.

Again, look up the empirical supporting details at the Center for Climate Communications at George Mason, in the citation above.

The five popular dividing prejudices that stopped actions on climate change in the last forty years are now receding in the public view. The prejudices of the past decades are eroding in the face of science, medicine, and the military, all realigned. We got early glimpses of these mega-changes in reviewing our work at bp and Trane for this book.

The dominant cultures fostering the maintenance of fossil fuels are being ferreted out in public forums, almost daily, and taxed heavily. Yet this is nothing as fast as the capital markets.

The investment firms—from Australia to Japan and Wall Street—are favoring a "just and rapid" transition. We see this most vividly in the States through the daily advances noted on Bloomberg news, and the actions of Michael Bloomberg himself in leading the Task Force on Climate-Related Financial Disclosures, a consortium on climate disclosures now involving more than a thousand key financial institutions. The capital markets have moved much faster than the national rule-makers in government, as a means of climate risk reduction and wealth protection.

EXPECT RESISTANCE TO THESE NEEDED CHANGES

In time, those resorting to a kind of reactionary resistance will be viewed as selfish and short-lived knuckleheads. Confirm this sense of social history by noting the alertness to climate in firms we reported on like bp and Trane. They have fired the knuckleheads and retrained talent open to climate competitiveness. New hires already believe in this mission.

Here is a point larger than the domain of this book: You can be assured that the mass momentum of history bypasses stubborn stupidities. What we referred to as the slow walking elephant of change does not often or for long step backwards.

Don't be distracted by the opponents of climate competitiveness. Instead, note the increase in the power of those speaking on behalf of the commons and the public commonwealth in the press, corporate, and military life. That is the real irrepressible development.

This is what I mean by changing views in the sea waves of the dominant, the emergent, and the reactionary parts of culture. Like the turbulent waters evident when the great Columbia River cascades down into a crash with the waters of the Pacific, it takes competing currents to make change.

When you study the grand history of our last forty years, flying over it like condors and eagles and hawks, you will see the chosen case companies in this book represent early exemplars that all firms and suppliers are now aligning with. This will help change everything, enabling a new age return back to basics in civics and the greater civil society.

HUMILITY AS THE BEST FINALE

While I believe my books align with the elephant marching forward, I am not arrogant in my certainties. Humility is my best finale.

While writing the chapters of this book in 2022 through the early months of 2023, while our world was still emerging from COVID and the pandemic, I felt humbled by this view of social history.

Many significant firms have begun to implement profitable solutions to carbon-and-capital-constraints. The principles of this book have been aligned with new corporate competitive principles. This has occurred more within the select corporate mansions I've seen firsthand, yet I know it is becoming widespread. But we have so much more to do in business and society.

To help visualize the skills required to install this new climate competitiveness narrative into your family and firm, pretend you are a chief sustainability officer.

Here are the skills my firm has advocated for CSOs over the last twenty years. We decided to use them as our case studies to support this narrative. Yet what matters is your firm's adoption and adaptation of these competitive principles summed up on page 141.

Gord Lambert, a key member of our firm, and the former top chief sustainability officer at Suncor Energy in Calgary, developed this list of seven summary attributes for our Corporate Affiliates like bp and Trane. We spend hundreds of hours in training beneath each bullet, to inform and to persuade some reluctant old world top executives. We supply the basics of this set of a thousand documents in this new narrative and book.

We live on the edge of a new age, an age where oil overproduction has led to a realignment of money, people, and rules. The changes I've noted in my work and firm are not those easily reported. The changes are carried forward by social force, not only by government rules. Instead, it was streams of each piece of the puzzle (business, government, wealth, the commonwealth) moving into a river torrent that can move rocks. This book centered its gravity on the four related legs of the elephant moving forward each day. It was a collective shift in attitudes and results that empowered many into these changes. The prejudices that kept many of us down are being seen through. I feel those rocks moving each week. With humility, I end in grateful witness of the torrents of today.

CSO CRITICAL COMPETENCIES AND CAPABILITIES

- **System thinker**—Values and engages diverse perspectives, expertise, and connections
- Central value proposition—**Engages Creative Tension** to drive better business and sustainability outcomes
    - Change agents of an expert caliber ... create Discomfort with Status Quo + inspiring Desired Future State outcomes

- **Ambassadors and CEO proxys**—external and internal
- **Collaboration orientation** vs *heroic* style leader—**must** empower, support, inspire and recognize others
    - Heroic leadership results in dis-empowering others ... and silo's the sustainability agenda and impact

- **Executive level business capabilities** ... with unique depth of expertise in sustainability (Not a sustainability expert with marginal business smarts)
    - Altruism is always possible as a sustainability motivator but not effective.

    - Shared Value Creation ... more compelling and powerful ... new business case model orientation

- **COS—Architects or co-Architects of Strategy but also Translators** ... to businesses, employees, investors and stakeholders
- **Intense Curiosity and Listening** ... internal and external ... **can navigate ambiguity**

There is so much talent in the world. It does not reside now only in the elite institutions, in the autocratic circles, or in the propagandist press.

And because this shared world of talent surrounds, your life will prove richer if you embrace the principles summed up in this fly over. There is time for your own protest song, and your role in this march towards a net zero world.

POSTSCRIPT

BILL NOVELLI

John Gardner, founder of Common Cause, the American citizen's advocacy group, once observed that "We're all faced with a series of great opportunities, brilliantly disguised as insoluble problems."

On the other hand, John McCain, the late U.S. Senator and presidential candidate, used to delight in commenting when the going got tough, "Remember, it's always darkest . . . before things go completely black!"

Today we are faced with the existential challenge of climate change. Which will it be? Gardner's brilliant opportunity for society to succeed, or McCain's black out?

Bruce Piasecki, in *Wealth and Climate Competitiveness: The New Narrative on Business and Society*, is a pragmatic optimist. He sees *opportunity*, but not without fighting for the changes we must achieve. Bruce has written before about the nexus of business and society. And now this important book lays out his basic premise: we *must* find a better balance—a proper ratio —between wealth (individual and corporate) and the commonwealth (society) to solve our climate issues and reinvent our energy infrastructure, our agriculture and our global transport.

In short, we need to get back to the basics. We have to solve the challenges before us regarding climate and capital allocation, and the conflict that has been created from the collision of business and society—of over-industrialization and climate havoc.

Who is going to pull this off? Who has the capability, courage and foresight? A few years ago, an article in the *Washington Post* proclaimed that there was a bacterium that was eating the oil from the enormous oil spill in the Gulf of Mexico. Sometime later a second article appeared announcing that there was no such bacterium. It would be nice, but no such miracles are going to rescue us. Bruce knows we must do it ourselves.

And that's the challenge underlying Bruce's book. He traces the arc of nineteenth-, twentieth-, and twenty-first-century petrochemical ascendance and wealth creation. As he notes, superabundant oil and related fossil fuels like gas and coal got in the way of basic civics. Our social contract faded in the age of oil and oil-generated wealth.

Over time, social movements, often driven in part by nonprofit organizations, got stronger, improved their change strategies and have been making a difference. They are buttressed by strong boards of directors, often hailing from the most generous and effective segments of the corporate sector. These movements also are benefiting from increasing diversity, and the environmental movement, once made up mostly of educated elites, is becoming more inclusive.

Bruce cites AARP, where I was the CEO. Like Bruce, I see social movements as key drivers of change. I called AARP a "warrior brand," and we pursued change at the macro level of social norm change as well as working at the grass roots to change individual behaviors.

What do social organizations and movements do to effect change? They rally public support; advocate for legislative, regulatory and legal changes: they work with the private sector in partnerships; and they seek system change (e.g., the workplace, health care, and education). All this is required in a creative realignment to tackle climate change, Piasecki explains.

Coupled with—and encouraged by—social movements, are the growing corporate trends in ESG (social, environmental, governance) and stakeholder capitalism, which Bruce calls social response capitalism in his books *World Inc* and *A New Way to Wealth*.

Bruce sits with me on a board I chair with Dr. Stephen Schneider, the Medical Consortium on Public Health and Climate. From these years serving that consortium we have advised Congress, the states and medical societies like the AMA, I know Bruce is a thinker in action, not a thinker only. I've admired his articulate pragmatism in action; informed by the historic lessons in this book before you.

WHY THIS BOOK MATTERS

In a nutshell, more and more companies are figuring out that they can incorporate social and environmental strategies into their core businesses. The result can be greater financial returns for stockholders as well as social and environmental value for the rest of society.

The growing effectiveness of social movements coupled with social response capitalism are presented in *Wealth and Climate Competitiveness* as important contributors to the needed balance between business and society and to attacking the ever-growing threat of climate change.

But none of this is going to bear fruit without public support. Where is public opinion in the climate debate? We know public attitudes can be fickle. People say they want less government, but more public services. They demand leadership from their public officials, but often pay little attention to the issues or even bother to vote. And with climate, like so many other issues, culture war partisanship influences public opinion.

These culture wars have exacerbated the tendency to revile government as the problem, rather than part of the solution to our social ills. Bruce disagrees. He points out that hating government is self-defeating. We need all sectors, working together, to find the answers.

Fortunately, as Bruce points out, the public is beginning to respond to the need for climate action. Piasecki quotes Professor Ed Maibach that some 58 percent of American voters, including 48 percent of Republican moderates, want President Biden to call a national emergency if Congress does not act. That documentation turns out to be a key pivot point in our recent social history, tipping the balance into action. This level of public opinion is what helped sway policy makers to pivot after decades of inaction, and pass the Inflation Reduction Act, as I write this.

Somehow Piasecki knew to write these new narratives in anticipation of the required next steps in this coming decade, and beyond. Change takes time for this massive transformation to clean energy, and Piasecki outlines the storyline.

In short, we know how to count votes. Yet to make all this advance fast enough, we need to move many voters and corporate leaders. They need now know social marketing, to launch what Piasecki calls "rock moving narratives" that count to a range of peoples. More is needed now in this decade to galvanize the public. In sum, things are moving in the right direction with this historic passage of the new federal legislation, devoting more than 400 billion to help people invest in climate solutions in their cars, homes, and electric dials. But we need further action by many along the lines of this book.

HE SAT ON THE CLINTON WHITE HOUSE ADVISORY COUNCIL ON CLIMATE AND TECHNOLOGY

Good things take time. Bruce calls for leadership—which is in short supply—in all sectors. He is a strong believer in leaders and heroes (read any of his five leader biographies, for instance). In action, Bruce has assembled with his staff and facilitated over fifty firms, into two-day achieving-results sessions—what he calls workshops. He sets before us an unusual group we might not think of on our own. This led the author to have a rich roller deck of influencers.

For example, in this new book, he looks at the Gates family. There is Bill Gates Senior, who wrote that we exist in a community that makes claims on all of us. Thinking that "it is all mine" violates this, and so we need a far-sighted notion of citizenship and the needs of business and society. Let us ask, "What can I give back?"

Bruce writes often of Benjamin Franklin, whom he considers a brilliant thinker and the first global citizen. Franklin, like Bruce, thought that social purpose was the way to wealth. Franklin advocated frugality, which Bruce interprets in modern terms. He calls it "competitive frugality" and sees it as a competitive advantage to frame wealth in the context of social value. This can enable us to progress in the marketplace, to tackle climate change, and to thrive over the rest of this century.

HEROES IN ACTION ARTICULATE PRODUCTIVE PROTEST SONGS

Bruce knows well that sometimes it is necessary to disrupt social order to achieve social change. So he presents us with Henry David Thoreau and his philosophy of civil disobedience, adhered to by Gandhi and Martin Luther King Jr., and the "good trouble" actions of John Lewis.

In short, we must act assertively to combat climate change. This is no time for idle contemplation. It reminds me of my favorite mantra: "problems worthy of attack, prove their worth by attacking back." These are the big, truly tough challenges—with climate change at the top of the list. We can't sit on our hands and wait for someone else to do the job.

Bruce is no tree-hugging socialist. He is instead a scholar, a successful businessperson, and a keen social observer. His roots, as he describes them, are based on working class values. I share his blue-collar background, and I know that when you stand up and call for great social change, as Bruce does in this book, you open yourself up to charges and criticisms of socialism and anti-capitalism. Bruce puts this to rest. He says he indeed has been called a socialist, but he is instead "a clear-headed capitalist and conventional investor in stocks for over fifty years." He adds an amusing comment: that he learned from none other than Karl Marx that he had to "own" the means of production (hence his successful company providing counsel to many major corporations).

A PARADOX IN PIASECKI'S WORKS

This book contains an interesting paradox, which is a Bruce Piasecki specialty. Yes, we must do more with less, he says. But at the same time, we need what he calls "enough excess" in a modern society. Excess?

Well, his prior book *A New Way to Wealth* dramatized what he called "social wealth in all its glory." In this book,

Piasecki goes further in asking "What is Enough?" Bruce says we do not thrive when our lives are "spare." We shouldn't withdraw from the "wealth" of the arts and of civilization. We don't want to saddle ourselves with draconian rules and policies. In essence, we need to live life fully and solve our existential problem of climate change.

Can we do it? Bruce thinks we can, and that our herculean task will be easier if we follow the paths outlined in this new book. The next image shows, in a sportive way, how Bruce thinks of change management. I talk about the need to fight; he talks about being like an elephant moving forward: stubborn and persistent, and alert to the sounds of the terrain.

He also asks a profound and related question for us to consider: how much is enough? In the context of needing "excess" in our lives to be fully alive, when and what is enough? This is important in striking the right balance between wealth and the commonwealth.

As Bruce points out, too much excess and lack of saying "enough" upsets the balance we must achieve. And without that balance, the rich get richer and the rest of society is left behind. It reminds me of the nanny philosopher, Mary Poppins, who said, "Enough is as good as a feast." We must find that elusive balance.

Finally, we must learn to share our wealth and our planet with coming generations. Bruce wants those who follow us—our children and grandchildren and generations still unborn—to become independent and wealthy in their own life. That requires a livable Earth.

In my own book, *Good Business*, I point out that when my youngest grandson, Victor, comes of age, many of the present coast lines, including major cities in the United States and other countries, could be under water, and severe heat could be unbearable around the world. We must act. To succeed, we need to accomplish Bruce's call to action: to find the right balance between wealth and commonwealth.

Our common future depends on it.

Bill Novelli is the former CEO of AARP and co-founder of Porter Novelli, the global public relations firm. He is a retired professor at Georgetown University's McDonough School of Business. His latest book is *Good Business: The Talk, Fight Win Way to Change the World*.

ANNOTATED BIBLIOGRAPHY

PREPARED BY IRA FELDMAN

I asked my longtime colleague, Ira Feldman (founder and chairman of Adaptation Leader) to prepare an annotated bibliography. I find Ira's work enormously useful. I hope you agree.

I. Prior Use of the Term "Climate Competitiveness"

Jonathan Lash and Fred Wellington, "Competitive Advantage on a Warming Planet" (2007)

> "In this article, the authors offer a systematic approach to mapping and responding to climate change risks. . . [They] propose a four-step process for responding to climate change risk: Quantify your company's carbon footprint, identify the risks and opportunities you face, adapt your business in response, and do it better than your competitors. Today's customers insist that the companies they support do their part to address climate change." https://hbr.org/2007/03/competitive-advantage-on-a-warming-planet

Accountability (2010)

The Climate Competitiveness Index 2010: National progress in the low carbon economy Summary for Decision-Makers (report prepared for UNEP)

> "A green economy brings with it not only the opportunity to reduce greenhouse gas emissions, but also to generate new jobs, new technologies and new businesses. This report underlines the move towards a green economy in different regions and helps to assess which regions are currently best placed to thrive in the low carbon econ-

omy of the future. . . . Developing the Climate Competitiveness Index and the accompanying analysis has also made us even more aware of shortcomings in the underlying data and the need to push for more robustness and comprehensiveness for the Index to become even more meaningful and applicable in the coming years." https://unfccc.int/files/adaptation/application/pdf/accountability_climate_competitiveness_index_2010_21042010.pdf

OECD (2010) "Climate change and competitiveness." (Remarks by Angel Gurria, OECD Secretary General, at Johns Hopkins School of Advanced International Studies.)

"[T] here are many challenges to build a comprehensive international framework to address climate change. But if domestically we are able to make progress in dealing with competitiveness concerns, this will take us a good way forward. We, at the OECD, with several decades of experience in dealing with climate change and a recent mandate to develop a Green Growth Strategy, are ready to continue contributing to inform the debate." https://www.oecd.org/env/cc/climatechangeandcompetitiveness.htm

World Bank (2016)
"A greener path to competitiveness: policies for climate action in industries and products"

"Although industry's threat to climate and the environment is clear, the business case for decarbonizing manufacturing—making it greener—is not. A new report from The World Bank Group, CLASP, and Carbon Trust, *A Greener Path to Competitiveness* offers recommendations and guidance on how companies and countries can stay competitive while implementing more climate-friendly technologies and strategies." https://www.worldbank.org/en/topic/competitiveness/publication/a-greener-path-to-competitiveness-policies-for-climate-action-in-industries-and-products

OECD (2018)
Issue Paper: "Green policies and firms' competitiveness"

"A major concern in the context of the green transition is the potential impacts of environmental policies, and of green growth policy packages more generally, on the competitiveness of companies affected by these regulations. Businesses and policy makers fear that, in a world characterised by integrated global value chains and capital flows, differences in the stringency of environmental policies across countries could shift pollution-intensive production capacity towards regions with less ambitious regulation . . . Many countries are concerned that their efforts to achieve carbon emission reductions will put their own carbon-intensive producers at a competitive disadvantage in the global economy, and such concerns are often used by policy makers as a justification for not introducing more ambitious environmental policies." https://www.oecd.org/greengrowth/GGSD_2018_Competitiveness%20Issue%20Paper_WEB.pdf

Trucost (2018) "Corporate Climate Competitiveness: Growing Your Business, Optimizing Investments, and Managing Costs."
"Because transitioning to a low-carbon economy presents companies with complex choices, Trucost developed the Green Transition Tool to simplify decision-making. The tool quantifies different ways to decrease fossil use, reduce exposure to carbon-related costs, and communicate alignment with the Task Force on Climate-related Disclosures (TCFD) recommendations. This paper examines three investment scenarios using the Green Transition Tool, consolidating publicly disclosed data—and compares the financial and environmental investment returns of each scenario." https://www.spglobal.com/marketintelligence/en/news-insights/research/corporate-rate-climate-competitiveness-growing-your-business-optimizing-investments-and-managing-costs

World Economic Forum (WEF) (2019)
"The Global Competitiveness Report"
"[T]he World Economic Forum introduced last year the new Global Competitiveness Index 4.0, a much-needed new economic compass, building on 40 years of experience of benchmarking the drivers of long-term competitiveness. The index is an annual yardstick for policy-makers to look beyond short-term and reactionary measures and to instead assess their progress against the full set of factors that determine productivity . . . The results of the GCI 4.0 in 2019 reveal that, on average, most economies continue to be far from the competitiveness "frontier"—

the aggregate ideal across all factors of competitiveness
. . . [I]t is crucial for economies to rely on fiscal policy,
structural reforms and public incentives to allocate more
resources towards the full range of factors of productivity to fully leverage the new opportunities provided by
the Fourth Industrial Revolution." https://www3.we-
forum.org/docs/WEF_TheGlobalCompetitivenessRe-
port2019.pdf

Hauke Ward, Jan Cristophe Steckel and Michael Jakob. "How global climate policy could affect competitiveness." Science Direct, 2019.
"A global uniform carbon price would be economically efficient and at the same time avoid 'carbon-leakage.' Still,
it will affect the competitiveness of specific industries,
economic activity and employment across countries. This
paper assesses short-term economic shocks following the
introduction of a global carbon price that would be in line
with the Paris Agreement . . . We find that impacts on industrial competitiveness are highly heterogeneous across
regions and economic sectors." https://www.sciencedi-
rect.com/science/article/pii/S0140988319303445

Agnieszka Karman, Andrzej Miszczuk and Urszula Bronisz. "Regional Climate Change Competitiveness—Modelling Approach."
Energies, 2021.
"The article deals with the competitiveness of regions in
the face of climate change. The aim was to present the
concept of measuring the Regional Climate Change
Competitiveness Index. We used a comparative and logical analysis of the concept of regional competitiveness and
heuristic conceptual methods to construct the index and
measurement scale . . . The conclusions of the research
confirm the possibility of applying the Regional Climate
Change Competitiveness Index in the economic analysis
and strategic planning. The presented model constitutes
one of the earliest tools for the evaluation of climate change
competitiveness at a regional level." https://www.mdpi.
com/1996-1073/14/12/3704

Yvonne Ruf and David Frans. "Climate action: A new competitiveness paradigm." Roland Berger, 2021.
"Action on climate change is no longer an optional or sec-
ond-rate consideration for companies; it must be priori-

tized as a core strategic pillar. Decarbonization is essential as a sign of a business' willingness to curb climate catastrophe . . . The study . . . addresses the urgent need for climate action and provides strategic recommendations on how companies can get an edge over the competition." https://www.rolandberger.com/en/Insights/Publications/Climate-action-A-new-competitiveness-paradigm.htm

Bundezfinanzministerium (BMF, the German Federal Finance Ministry) (2021)
"Steps towards an alliance for climate, competitiveness and industry—building blocks of a cooperative and open climate club."

"Practically all industrialised countries and emerging economies are facing the same overarching challenges: achieving the decarbonisation of the economy requires a massive technological effort. This can be tackled most efficiently together by means of international cooperation. While many countries are ramping up their efforts at the national (or European) level, we still lack a protective international framework . . . that would keep climate policy pioneers from being at a disadvantage in the international marketplace . . . It is clear that economies can only remain viable in the long term if there is an ambitious reduction in greenhouse gas emissions. At the same time, high climate standards should not place countries at a competitive disadvantage in the short or medium term, causing important industries to shift abroad." https://www.bundesfinanzministerium.de/Content/EN/Downloads/Climate-Action/key-issues-paper-international-climate-club.pdf?__blob=publicationFile&v=4

Toon Vandyck, Matthias Weitzel, et al. "Climate policy design, competitiveness and income distribution: A macro-micro assessment for 11 EU countries." Science Direct, 2021.

"Concerns about industry competitiveness and distributional impacts can deter ambitious climate policies. Typically, these issues are studied separately, without giving much attention to the interaction between the two. Here, we explore how carbon leakage reduction measures affect distributional outcomes across households within 11 European countries . . . While these findings suggest a competitiveness-equity trade-off, the results also show that . . . there is room for policy to reconcile competitiveness and equity concerns." https://www.sciencedirect.com/science/article/pii/S0140988321004151

Climate Strategies Poland Foundation, CDP & Germanwatch (2022)
"Corporate Climate Competitiveness Guide."

"This report has been prepared in the form of a comprehensive guide on climate competitiveness, addressed to the owners, supervisory and management board members, as well as the managers of medium and large companies. The study also aims to provide comprehensive knowledge to audiences who have not encountered any issues related to the carbon footprint, climate strategies, or issues related to the energy transition so far." https://climateandstrategy.com/the-corporate-climate-competitiveness-guide/

Business Roundtable (2021)
"A Call to Action from the Global Business Community: Global Businesses Support Climate Action that Enhances Competitiveness"

"Companies across the world have made climate action central to their strategies. Many of the companies we represent are setting climate targets and working towards net zero emissions. To get there, they are boosting energy efficiency, scaling up the generation and use of renewable energy, and integrating greenhouse gas (GHG) emissions reduction, resilience and adaptation strategies into the hearts of their business plans. The urgency and scale of the climate challenge is difficult to overstate. Yet the transformation of the global economy that it demands also presents an enormous and unprecedented opportunity for companies and citizens to achieve more sustainable prosperity." https://www.businessroundtable.org/a-call-to-action-from-the-global-business-community-global-businesses-support-climate-action-that-enhances-competitiveness

Information Technology & Innovation Foundation (2021)
"Clean and Competitive: Opportunities for U.S. Manufacturing Leadership in the Global-Low Carbon Economy"

"The United States needs an integrated national strategy to address the twin challenges of bolstering its manufacturing sector and averting climate change. Timely federal RD&D and deployment policies targeted to specific manufacturing industries could create comparative advantage, expanding domestic investment and employment." https://itif.org/publications/2021/06/21/clean-and-competitive-opportunities-us-manufacturing-leadership-global-low/

Economics Observatory (2022)
"How are climate change policies affecting firms' competitiveness?"

"Policies to tackle climate change can impose costs on firms, especially those with high emissions of greenhouse gases, potentially reducing their competitiveness in global markets. Such measures can also encourage innovation and provide opportunities for growth." https://www.economicsobservatory.com/how-are-climate-change-policies-affecting-firms-competitiveness

Center for Climate and Energy Solutions (C2ES) (2021)
"The Business Case for Climate Action"

"Leading companies recognize climate change as both a risk and an opportunity. A growing number are taking steps to strengthen their resilience to climate impacts, reduce their greenhouse gas emissions, produce innovative low-carbon technologies, and support policies enabling a smooth transition to a low-carbon economy." https://www.c2es.org/content/the-business-case-for-climate-action/

II. Key background materials

The Paris Climate Agreement (2015)

"The Paris Agreement is a legally binding international treaty on climate change. It was adopted by 196 Parties at the UN Climate Change Conference (COP21) in Paris, France, on 12 December 2015. It entered into force on 4 November 2016. Its overarching goal is to hold "the increase in the global average temperature to well below 2°C above pre-industrial levels" and pursue efforts "to limit the temperature increase to 1.5°C above pre-industrial levels." Full text available at: https://unfccc.int/process/conferences/pastconferences/paris-climate-change-conference-november-2015/paris-agreement

IPCC (2023)
AR6 "Summary for Policymakers" report

> "The Synthesis Report is based on the content of the three Working Groups Assessment Reports: WGI—The Physical Science Basis, WGII—Impacts, Adaptation and Vulnerability, WGIII—Mitigation of Climate Change, and the three Special Reports: Global Warming of 1.5°C, Climate Change and Land, The Ocean and Cryosphere in a Changing Climate. [It] consists of an introduction and three main sections arranged by timeframes. The first section, 'Current Status and Trends,' covers the historical and present period. The second section, 'Long-term Climate and Development Futures,' addresses projected futures up to 2100 and beyond. The final section is 'Near-term Responses in a Changing Climate,' considers current international policy timeframes, and the time interval between now and 2030–2040." https://report.ipcc.ch/ar6syr/pdf/IPCC_AR6_SYR_SPM.pdf

US National Climate Assessment (2019)

> "The Fourth National Climate Assessment (NCA4), completed in November 2018, is a comprehensive and authoritative report on climate change and its impacts in the United States. The U.S. Global Change Research Program (USGCRP) was established by Presidential initiative in 1989 and mandated by Congress in the Global Change Research Act (GCRA) of 1990. Its mandate is to develop and coordinate 'a comprehensive and integrated United States research program which will assist the Nation and the world to understand, assess, predict, and respond to human-induced and natural processes of global change.' USGCRP comprises 14 Federal agencies that conduct or use research on global change and its impacts on society." https://www.globalchange.gov/nca4

UNEP (2022)
Emissions Gap report 2022: "The Closing Window"

> "As growing climate change impacts are experienced across the globe, the message that greenhouse gas emissions must fall is unambiguous. Yet the *Emissions Gap Report (EGR) 2022: The Closing Window—Climate crisis calls for rapid transformation of societies* finds that the internation-

al community is falling far short of the Paris goals, with no credible pathway to 1.5°C in place. Only an urgent system-wide transformation can avoid climate disaster." https://www.unep.org/resources/emissions-gap-report-2022

United Nations (2012)
"The Future We Want"—Declaration of the UN Conference on Sustainable Development, Rio

"The Future We Want is the declaration on sustainable development and a green economy adopted at the UN Conference on Sustainable Development in Rio on June 19, 2012. The Declaration includes broad sustainability objectives within themes of Poverty Eradication, Food Security and Sustainable Agriculture, Energy, Sustainable Transport, Sustainable Cities, Health and Population and Promoting Full and Productive Employment. It calls for the negotiation and adoption of internationally agreed Sustainable Development Goals by end 2014. It also calls for a UN resolution strengthening and consolidating UNEP both financially and institutionally so that it can better disseminate environmental information and provide capacity building for countries." The full text of the Rio+20 outcome document is available at: https://www.eea.europa.eu/policy-documents/the-future-we-want-2013declaration

United Nations (2015)
"Transforming Our World: the 2030 Agenda for Sustainable Development"

"Transforming our world: the 2030 Agenda for Sustainable Development with its 17 SDGs was adopted at the UN Sustainable Development Summit in New York in September 2015 . . . Every year, the UN Secretary General presents an annual SDG Progress report, which is developed in cooperation with the UN System, and based on the global indicator framework and data produced by national statistical systems and information collected at the regional level . . . Additionally, the Global Sustainable Development Report is produced once every four years to inform the quadrennial SDG review deliberations at the General Assembly. It is written by an Independent Group of Scientists appointed by the Secretary-General." https://sdgs.un.org/2030agenda

James Hanson 1988 testimony to US Senate
"Statement of Dr. James Hansen, NASA Goddard Institute"

> James Hansen is known as the "Father of Global Warming" chiefly because of his 1988 testimony before the U.S. Senate, in which he announced that " . . . the greenhouse effect has been detected, and is changing our climate now." A transcribed excerpt of his remarks "Greenhouse Effect and Global Climate Change" at the June 23, 1988, hearing before the Committee on Energy and Natural Resources of the United States Senate is available at: https://pulitzercenter.org/sites/default/files/june_23_1988_senate_hearing_1.pdf

III. Recent popular books related to climate change

Elizabeth Kolbert. *The Sixth Extinction: An Unnatural History*. New York: Macmillan, 2015.

> *"New Yorker* writer Elizabeth Kolbert tells us why and how human beings have altered life on the planet in a way no species has before. [T]here have been Five mass extinctions, when the diversity of life on earth suddenly and dramatically contracted . . . This time around, the cataclysm is us." https://us.macmillan.com/books/9781250062185/thesixthextinction

Naomi Klein. *This Changes Everything*. New York: Simon & Schuster, 2015.

> "In *This Changes Everything* Naomi Klein argues that climate change isn't just another issue to be neatly filed between taxes and health care. It's an alarm that calls us to fix an economic system that is already failing us in many ways." https://www.simonandschuster.com/books/This-Changes-Everything/Naomi-Klein/9781451697391

David Wallace-Wells. *The Uninhabitable Earth: Life After Warming*. New York: Random House 2019.

> "The Uninhabitable Earth is both a travelogue of the near future and a meditation on how that future will look to those living through it—the ways that warming promises to transform global politics, the meaning of technology and nature in the modern world, the sustainability of capitalism and the trajectory of human progress." https://

www.penguinrandomhouse.com/books/586541/the-un-inhabitable-earth-by-david-wallace-wells/

John Doerr. *Speed & Scale: An Action Plan for Solving Our Climate Crisis Now*. New York: Random House, 2021.

"With clear-eyed realism and an engineer's precision, Doerr lays out the practical actions, global ambitions, and economic investments we need to avert climate catastrophe. Guided by real-world solutions, *Speed & Scale* features unprecedented, firsthand accounts from climate leaders . . . and dozens of other intrepid policymakers, innovators, and scientists." https://www.penguinrandomhouse.com/books/688191/speed-and-scale-by-john-doerr/

Bill Gates. *How to Avoid a Climate Disaster: The Solutions We Have and the Breakthroughs We Need*. New York: Knopf, 2021.

"Bill Gates sets out a wide-ranging, practical—and accessible—plan for how the world can get to zero greenhouse gas emissions in time to avoid a climate catastrophe . . . In this book, he not only explains why we need to work toward net-zero emissions of greenhouse gases, but also details what we need to do to achieve this profoundly important goal." https://www.penguinrandomhouse.com/books/633968/how-to-avoid-a-climate-disaster-by-bill-gates/

Kim Stanley Robinson. *The Ministry for the Future: A Novel*. New York: Hachette Book Group, 2020.

"*The Ministry for the Future* is a masterpiece of the imagination, using fictional eyewitness accounts to tell the story of how climate change will affect us all. Its setting is not a desolate, postapocalyptic world, but a future that is almost upon us . . . [T]his extraordinary novel from visionary science fiction writer Kim Stanley Robinson will change the way you think about the climate crisis." https://www.hachettebookgroup.com/titles/kim-stanley-robinson/the-ministry-for-the-future/9780316300131/

IV. Selected climate topics relevant to business and finance

Business generally

Michael Bloomberg, Henry Paulson and Tom Steyer. "Risky

Business: The Economic Risks of Climate Change in the United States." Risky Business Project, 2014.

> "A Climate Risk Assessment for the United States identifies the economic risks posed by a changing climate. The U.S. will likely face the effects of human-induced climate change including rising seas and more frequent bouts of extreme heat. The report identifies striking economic impacts from climate change, from the near-term to the end of the century across all 50 U.S. states." http://riskybusiness.org/report/national/

Mark Trexler & Laura Kosloff. *The Changing Profile of Corporate Climate Change Risk*. Oxfordshire, UK: Routledge, 2012.

> "As national and global policy to materially reduce climate change is delayed, it is business-prudent to assume that the level of climate risk is increasing . . . Should physical impacts of climate change manifest in dramatic ways . . . [t]hese conditions create a complex and shifting business risk environment, and most companies either overlook or substantially underestimate key climate risks." https://www.routledge.com/The-Changing-Profile-of-Corporate-Climate-Change-Risk/Trexler-Kosloff/p/book/9781909293007

Christopher Wright and Daniel Nyberg. *Climate Change, Capitalism, and Corporations: Processes of Creative Self-Destruction*. Cambridge: Cambridge University Press, 2015.

> "This book explores the complex relationship that the corporate world has with climate change and examines the central role of corporations in shaping political and social responses to the climate crisis. ... This book moves beyond descriptive and normative approaches to provide a sociologically and critically informed theory of corporate responses to climate change." https://www.cambridge.org/core/books/climate-change-capitalism-and-corporations/9FD46E7FF5F-9FE71508831A23D43DEE0

Jorge Rivera. *Business Adaptation to Climate Change*. Cambridge: Cambridge University Press, 2022.

> "This book seeks to advance the understanding of how businesses may adapt to climate change trends. Specifically, it focuses on two general research questions: First-

ly, how do businesses adapt to chronic slow-onset nature adversity conditions linked to climate change? Secondly, how do firms adapt to weather-related natural disasters exacerbated by climate change?" https://www.cambridge. org/core/books/business-adaptation-to-climate-change/ 28B8E17A77161222A6CA797D7708956F

Terry Anderson. *Adapt and Be Adept: Market Responses to Climate Change.* Sanford, CA:
Hoover Institution Press, 2021.
> "How can markets help us address the challenges of climate change? Most current climate policies require hard-to-enforce collective action and focus on reducing greenhouse gases rather than adapting to their negative effects. [In this book] Terry L. Anderson brings together essays by nine leading policy analysts who argue that adaptive actions can typically deliver much more, faster, and more cheaply than any realistic climate policy." https://hooverpress.bookstore.ipgbook. com/adapt-and-be-adept-products-9780817924553.php

McKenzie Funk. *The Windfall: The Booming Business of Global Warming.* New York: Penguin Books, 2015.
> "Funk shows us that the best way to understand the catastrophe of global warming is to see it through the eyes of those who see it most clearly—as a market opportunity. Global warming's physical impacts can be separated into three broad categories: melt, drought, and deluge. Funk . . . profile[s] entrepreneurial people who see in each of these forces a potential windfall." https://www.penguinrandomhouse. com/books/303480/windfall-by-mckenzie-funk/

Insurance and climate adaptation
M. Beck, O. Quast and K. Pfliegner. "Ecosystem-based Adaptation and Insurance: Success, Challenges and Opportunities."
> "[F]ew fully integrated Climate Risk Finance & Insurance (CRFI) & EbA products . . . currently exist . . . That said, there are many common interests and significant opportunities which could help improve integration of CFRI with EbA and more broadly Nature-based Solutions (NbS), which will lead to innovations beneficial to both sectors and, most importantly, to improved resilience outcomes for vulnerable people and for nature." https://www.adaptationcommunity.net/wp-content/uploads/2019/11/EbA_insurance_publication_2019_web.pdf

Governance & policy

Michael P. Vandenbergh and Jonathan Gilligan. *Beyond Politics: The Private Governance Response to Climate Change.* Cambridge: Cambridge University Press, 2017.

> "Private sector action provides one of the most promising opportunities to reduce the risks of climate change, buying time while governments move slowly or even oppose climate mitigation. Starting with the insight that much of the resistance to climate mitigation is grounded in concern about the role of government, this books draws on law, policy, social science, and climate science to demonstrate how private initiatives are already bypassing government inaction in the US and around the globe." https://www.cambridge.org/core/books/beyond-politics/5B7D5AB62C63D54EC35CBB95D72A47D9

Climate change and Innovation

Stelvia Matos, Eric Viardot, Benjamin K. Sovacool, Frank W. Geels and Yu Xiong. "Innovation and climate change: A review and introduction to the special issue." *Technovation*, 117:102612, 2022.

> "While innovation is expected to play a major role in decarbonization, the development and diffusion of low-carbon technologies are too slow in most sectors and countries to stabilize the climate. In this introductory paper . . . we review selected innovation studies literature, reflect on historical trends and insights, and cast light on future research on innovation and climate change." https://www.sciencedirect.com/science/article/pii/S0166497222001596

Climate communications

M. Ballew, M. Verner, J. Carman, S. Rosenthal, E. Maibach, J. Kotcher and A. Leiserowitz. "Global Warming's Six Americas across age, race/ethnicity, and gender." Yale University and George Mason University: Program on Climate Change Communication, 2023.

> "The Global Warming's Six Americas framework is an audience segmentation approach to understanding the spectrum of people's responses to global warming . . . In this analysis, we assess demographic group differences in climate opinion—and how they interact—by investigating Global Warming's Six Americas across age, race/ethnicity, and gender. We combine data from the six latest waves of our Climate Change in the Ameri-

can Mind surveys spanning from 2020-2022." https://
climatecommunication.yale.edu/publications/global-
warmings-six-americas-age-race-ethnicity-gender/

Climate change science
The Economist, 2010. Briefing: The clouds of unknowing
"The defenders of the consensus tend to stress the general consilience of their efforts—the way that data, theory and modelling back each other up. Doubters see this as a thoroughgoing version of 'confirmation bias,' the tendency people have to select the evidence that agrees with their original outlook. But although there is undoubtedly some degree of that . . . there is still genuine power to the way different arguments and datasets in climate science tend to reinforce each other." https://www.economist.com/briefing/2010/03/18/the-clouds-of-unknowing

The Economist (2022)
Briefing: "The world is going to miss the totemic 1.5C target"
"In the years since Paris, the 1.5°C target went from something to be pursued to something totemised. A stretch goal has been widely treated as a paramount one . . . [S]eeing the target treated as attainable has led many to believe that added political will and increasingly fervent denunciations of fossil fuels can get the range of the possible all the way down to a warming of just 1.5°C . . . This year, as the climate world meets in Sharm el-Sheikh . . . for COP 27, it would be far better to acknowledge that 1.5 is dead." https://www.economist.com/interactive/briefing/2022/11/05/the-world-is-going-to-miss-the-totemic-1-5c-climate-target

Kerry Emanuel. *What We Know About Climate Change*, Updated Edition. MIT Press, 2018.
"In this updated edition of his authoritative book, MIT atmospheric scientist Kerry Emanuel outlines the basic science of global warming and how the current consensus has emerged. Although it is impossible to predict exactly when the most dramatic effects of global warming will be felt, he argues, we can be confident that we face real dangers . . . Emanuel calls for urgent action to reduce greenhouse gases and criticizes the media for downplaying the dangers of global warming." https://mitpress.mit.edu/9780262535915/what-we-know-about-climate-change/

Climate change scenarios

Nardia Haigh. *Scenario Planning for Climate Change: A Guide for Strategists*. Oxfordshire: Routledge, 2019.

> "Uncertainty about access to resources, unanticipated weather events, rapidly changing market conditions and potential social unrest is felt across all business and industry sectors. This book sets out an engaging step-by-step scenario-planning method that executives, Board members, managers and consultants can follow to develop a long-term strategy for climate change tailored for their business." https://www.routledge.com/Scenario-Planning-for-Climate-Change-A-Guide-for-Strategists/Haigh/p/book/9781138498402

Geoengineering, carbon capture

Oliver Morton. *The Planet Remade: How Geoengineering Could Change the World*. Princeton University Press, 2015.

> "[A] small but increasingly influential group of scientists is exploring proposals for planned human intervention in the climate system: a stratospheric veil against the sun, the cultivation of photosynthetic plankton, fleets of unmanned ships seeding the clouds. These are the technologies of geoengineering—and as Oliver Morton argues in this visionary book, it would be as irresponsible to ignore them as it would be foolish to see them as a simple solution to the problem." https://press.princeton.edu/books/hardcover/9780691148250/the-planet-remade

Wil Burns, David Dana and Simon Nicholson, eds. *Climate Geoengineering: Science, Law and Governance.* Berlin: Springer Nature, 2021.

> "This volume . . . explore[s] scientific, political and legal issues associated with the emerging field of climate geoengineering . . . The sobering reality of the disconnect between the resolve of the world community to effectively address climate change, and what actually needs to be done, has led to increasing impetus for consideration of a suite of approaches collectively known as 'climate geoengineering,' [and] has transformed climate geoengineering from a fringe concept to a potentially mainstream policy option within the past decade." https://link.springer.com/book/10.1007/978-3-030-72372-9

Climate as a threat multiplier

Sherri Goodman and Pauline Baudu. Briefer: "Climate Change as

a 'Threat Multiplier': History, Uses and Future of the Concept."
The Center for Climate & Security, 2023.

> "Threat multiplier' has become a widely used term by scholars and practitioners to describe climate change implications for security in both the policy realm and climate-security literature . . . It captures how climate change effects interact with and have the potential to exacerbate pre-existing threats and other drivers of instability to contribute to security risks . . . Its use has also been described as 'one of the most prominent ways in which the security implications of climate change have been understood.'" https://climateandsecurity. org/2023/01/briefer-climate-change-as-a-threat-multiplier-history-uses-and-future-of-the-concept/

Threat of civilizational collapse

Jem Bendell and Rupert Read, eds. *Deep Adaptation: Navigating the Realities of Climate Chaos.*
Polity, 2021.

> "'Deep adaptation' refers to the personal and collective changes that might help us to prepare for— and live with—a climate-influenced breakdown or collapse of our societies . . . This is the first book to show how professionals across different sectors are beginning to incorporate the acceptance of likely or unfolding societal breakdown into their work and lives. They do not assume that our current economic, social and political systems can be made resilient in the face of climate change." https://www.wiley.com/ en-us/Deep+Adaptation:+Navigating+the+Realities+ of+Climate+Chaos-p-9781509546831

Daniel Steel, C. Tyler DesRoches and Kian Mintz-Woo. "Climate change and the threat to civilization." *PNAS*, 2022.

> "Here we call for treating the mechanisms and uncertainties associated with climate collapse as a critically important topic for scientific inquiry. Doing so requires clarifying what 'civilization collapse' means and explaining how it connects to topics addressed in climate science, such as increased risks from both fast- and slow-onset extreme weather events. This kind of information, we claim, is crucial for the public and for policymakers alike, for whom climate collapse may be a serious concern." https://www.pnas.org/doi/10.1073/pnas.2210525119